AMJAD NASSER

Shepherd of Solitude

Shepherd of Solitude is Amjad Nasser's first collection in English translation. Born in al-Turra, Jordan, in 1955, he is a major contributor to today's Arab poetry scene and has published eight volumes of poetry and two travel memoirs, *Flight of Wings* (1998) and *Under More than One Sky* (2002). He is managing editor and cultural editor of *Al-Quds Al-Arabi* daily newspaper. A selection of his poetry was published in French translation, *Ascension de l'amant*, with a Foreword by Adonis, (1998), also one in Italian (2001) and one in Spanish (2002).

Khaled Mattawa is the author of four books of poetry, *Ismailia Eclipse* (1996), *Zodiac of Echoes* (2003), *Amorisco* (2008), and *Tocqueville* (forthcoming 2010). He has translated seven volumes of contemporary Arabic poetry and co-edited two anthologies of Arab American literature. His awards include Guggenheim and Alfred Hodder fellowships, three Pushcart Prizes and a PEN translation prize. He teaches in the MFA in Creative Writing Program at the University of Michigan, Ann Arbor.

AMJAD NASSER

Shepherd of Solitude

Selected Poems 1979–2004

translated from the Arabic
and introduced by Khaled Mattawa

Banipal Books
2009

First published in the UK by Banipal Books, London 2009

Original works copyright © 2009 Amjad Nasser
Translation copyright © 2009 Khaled Mattawa

The poems in this collection were translated by Khaled Mattawa from *Al-A'mal al-Shi'ria [Collected Poetic Works]*, Amman: Al-Muassassa al-Arabiya lil-Dirasat wal-Nashr, 2002, and *Hayatuka Sardun Mutaqata [Life Like A Broken Narrative]*, Beirut: Riad el-Rayyes, 2004

The moral right of Amjad Nasser to be identified as the original author of these works and of Khaled Mattawa as the translator of these works has been asserted in accordance with the Copyright, Designs and Patents Act, 1988. All rights reserved. No part of this book may be reproduced in any form or by any means without the prior written permission of the publisher

A CIP record for this book is available in the British Library
ISBN 978-0-9549666-8-3

Banipal Books
1 Gough Square, LONDON EC4A 3DE, UK
www.banipal.co.uk

Set in Bembo
Printed and bound in the UK

For Hind,
today and tomorrow

ACKNOWLEDGEMENTS

The translator is indebted to Nava Etshalom for combing through this manuscript and offering countless helpful suggestions. Thanks also to Kristie Kachler for her help in refining this manuscript.

Finally, thanks to the editors of these magazines for publishing some of the poems in this manuscript in their journals:

Banipal: "Souvenir", "Dog's Tail", "Something Like Anger, Like Betrayal", Preparing for Flight", "A Resemblance", "Puppy Dog,", "The Phases of the Moon in London" and "An Ordinary Conversation about Cancer".

Diode: "Gates to the Sky, but They are Narrow," and "A Song and Three Questions."

Redivider: "Textile Workers," "One Flower," "Chance," "1955."

Shepherd of Solitude

CONTENTS

Introduction 1

Praise for Another Café, 1979
Gates to the Sky, but they are Narrow . . .26
Textile Workers .30
Praise for Another Café 32
Viva 36
Concrete 40
A Song and Three Questions 42

Climbing the Mountain Since Gilead, 1981
Song 46
Places 47
Excerpts from the Body's Sura 48
Lampoon 50
Grandfather 52
Wings 53
Fatigue 54
One Flower 55
Shirts 57

The Bleating of Copper 60
To You, Howdahs! 61

Shepherds of Solitude, 1986
Exile 63
Overdue Conversation 65
Bent Branches .68
Loneliness 70
Fever 72
Daily Occurrence 73
Once upon an Evening in a Café 74
Wrong Impressions 76
Shepherds of Solitude 78

The Strangers Arrive, 1990
Chance 90
The Strangers Arrive 91
The Impending Hour 95
1955 97
Lines to Joseph 99
Once upon a Time on an Island 100

Joy to All Who See You, 1994
Invocation for Entering the House 102
The Scent Reminds 103
A Rose of Black Lace 107
Invocation 112
The Lover's Ascent 113

Ascent of Breath, 1997
Farewell to Granada 122
Slant of Day 124
A Dusk Foretold 129
Ascent of Breath 134

Life Like A Broken Narrative, 2004
The House After Her Death 143
Old Radio 145
A Young Woman in Costa Café 147
Seven Bridges 149
Souvenir 152
A Ring from Kairouan 153
Dog's Tail 156
Something Like Anger, Like Betrayal . . .157
Preparing for Flight 160
A Resemblance 163
Puppy Dog 165
The Phases of the Moon in London . . .167
An Ordinary Conversation about Cancer 169
Neighbours .172
The Stars of London 174

INTRODUCTION

SHEPHERD OF MANY SOLITUDES

I

Individuals from contemporary Arab societies soon come to realize that identity is not innate and singular, but composite and layered. As soon we approach adult consciousness, we realize that the selves we harbor come in various colors and stripes and shapes. There's the self we of home where we are the youngest, the oldest, the girl or boy, and where our oedipal tensions are played out. Then there's the self of our character, our personal inclinations, the self that causes us to be doggedly loyal or selfish, hot-tempered or even-keeled, tender or cold. There's the self of our tribe, class, city, village, or neighborhood. Modern educational systems, wars, and international sports competitions instill a national self within us. And out of the chants and incense smoke of communal worship another self begins to inhabit us. Finally, there's the pan-national self, the sense of belonging found in the Arabic language, history and civilization. And beyond the selves we know and the ones we project, there's the self that seems to operate independently of us and that we sometimes catch a glimpse of in storefront windows or fractured mirrors. This flock of selves demands more effort to manage in times of political and social tension; it tends to increase in number and become more conflicted if one were to become dislocated or forced into exile. Perhaps people from the Arab world are no different in this regard from others elsewhere. Reading the region's history, we quickly learn that the search for identity has been intense in the Arab world for the last two centuries. Individuals and whole societies have been engaged in herding a flock of drives and hopes, sad histories and relentless legends, romanticized memories and necessary fabrications, frequent desertions and even more frequent reunions.

It is perhaps for this reason that the word "shepherd" resonates throughout Amjad Nasser's poetry. One can even say the word haunts his poems. A citizen of Jordan, Nasser was raised among the recently settled tribal peoples of the northern Arabian peninsula, the site of legendary battles over grazing rights. Amjad Nasser was Born in 1955 in the town of Mafraq. It should be noted that the name of Amjad's birth city, as if to suggest the continuous movement of its people, means "junction" or "intersection." It should also be noted that Amjad Nasser is a pseudonym he adopted upon deciding to become a poet and consequently leaving his hometown for good. He lived briefly in the sleepy urban setting of Amman then moved on to the cosmopolitanism of Beirut's civil war during which he published his first two books in 1979 and 1981. Among the thousands of intellectuals who had supported the Palestinian cause, he left Beirut after the Israeli invasion of Lebanon in 1982. He then lived in Cyprus for a few years during the decade when that island nation served as a transitional capital of Arab culture in exile. Nasser settled in London in 1987 where he still lives and works as the cultural editor for the daily newspaper Al-Quds Al-Arabi.

Nasser's publications include seven books of poetry: *Madeeh li-Maqha Akhar [Praise for Another Café]*, 1979; *Mundhu Jil'ad Kana Yas'adul Jabal [Climbing the Mountain Since Gilead]*, 1981; *Ru'at Al-Uzlah [Shepherds of Solitude]*, 1986; *Wussul Al-Ghurabaa [The Strangers Arrive]*, 1990; *Sarra Man Ra-aak [Joy to All Who See You]*, 1994; *Murtaqa Al-Anfas [Ascent of Breath]*, 1997; *Hayatuka Sardun Mutaqata [Life Like A Broken Narrative]*, 2004. He also authored two books of travel memoirs, *Khabtul Al-Ajniha [The Flapping of Wings]*, 1995, and *Tahta Akthar Min Samaa [Under More Than One Sky]*, 2002.

II

Nasser began to write during a self-conscious era in Arabic letters. Arabic poetry had seen its first truly revolutionary break from its very long past and was on the cusp of another by the time he started. After some pioneering work in Egypt and Lebanon, the first transformation came from Iraq in the late 1940's with the work of Nazik Al-Malaika and Badr Shakir Al-Sayyab. Both poets, and generations of poets that followed, abandoned the two-hemistich line and its requisite monorhyme. Poetry can be written in a combination of short and long lines with various rhyme combinations, the new poets demonstrated in the 1950's. They alternately demonstrated discipline by sticking to one metrical foot in a given poem. Poetry in the *taf'ila* mode, as it became to be known, maintained a musical quality, but granted its composers greater versatility in pacing than the classical mode. The *taf'ila* poetry brought a sense of newness to Arabic verse, allowing poets to incorporate subjects and allusions never before addressed. As such it helped secularize Arabic literature further releasing it from its confinement to Islamic allegiance and allusions and allowing it to rove and range among all the world's cultural referents.

Within two decades of its emergence, the *taf'ila* itself came under attack for being too melodramatic, false, and superficial. The *taf'ila* may have failed for two contrary purposes. Its major influence was Anglophone Modernism, especially the work of T S Eliot. Interestingly, the critique of *taf'ila* poetry that began in the late 1960's sounded very similar to that levelled on Eliot by his detractors, mainly William Carlos Williams and the

Beats. The *tafi'la* mode's emphasis on musicality made it possible to re-write the same old sentiments without challenging them, allowing traditional ideas to have a modern veneer while maintaining their conservative core. Secondly, the emphasis on obscure symbols and allusions in *taf'ila* poetry, in the hands of its high-minded poets, made it elitist and withdrawn. Furthermore, instead of opening the door for more renewal, *taf'ila* was quickly adopted by the establishment. Doctrinaire nationalists and socialists saw in it a way to connect to the masses and to help guide and control them, and pro-Western elitists saw in it an Arabic equivalent to the Western high Modernist writings they had been nurtured on. Such strictures left a great range of experiences unaddressed. By the late 1960's a new generation of poets began to veer away from *taf'ila*.

A later generation writing in the 1970's did not even attempt to write in any metered or rhymed verse, be it modern or classical. For these poets the quest was the same as it has ever been: they wanted to write poetry that was not adorned by overwrought music and delicacy, or by formality and collective sentiments. From hereon the Arab poet faced the page and wrote out of his lived experience and about it. He did not wish to uplift the nation or rouse it to fight, especially since the nation had been defeated partly due to grave shortcomings. Often enough the poet wrote of his alienation, his desire for flight, and longings for personal bonds and fulfillment. He, and increasingly she, did not think that these thoughts ought to proceed to the bounce of regular meter, but ought to demand a greater attentiveness, the one we devote to compressed, lyrical prose.

III

Armed with these discoveries, convictions, and aspirations, Amjad Nasser began to write in earnest in the mid-1970's. Let's take these few lines from Amjad's beginnings and witness him struggle with the position of the poet speaker. We'll address how the poem concludes, for now let's take a look at how it starts off:

> I will not defile my face feigning optimism.
> I will spread the plank of my chest for the birds
> coming from the dessert and the sea, and I will exhale
> a bundle of living smoke. Then I will stop speaking.

Our poet is taking a position against heroism in poetry and its promise of victory. For Nasser to feign optimism is to defile one's face, something he, who wants to be true to himself and who wants to keep his sense of identity in tact, would not do. He would prefer offer himself to scavenging birds than betray the truth as he knows it.

But what to make of the line "I will exhale/a bundle of living smoke." When would the poet do that? And what is a bundle of smoke exactly? Is the smoke itself an utterance since the poet says he will "stop speaking" later. The beginning of the poem achieves one thing successfully; it promises us honest self-assessment. Still, the poet has not freed himself from bravado. The dramatic nature of these lines hearkens to the same tone of the poet hero that our poet is trying to avoid. How will this conflict between tone and purpose resolve itself? Now let's listen to these lines from the end of the poem:

> In seconds, the scene takes shape:
> leather bags of different sizes
> and different contents,
> faces that go long
> and cloud up,
> features that take the shape of cramped muscles.
> The train heads north or south.
> No difference.
> The long whistles
> become a thin, agitated
> thread.
> And the scene folds upon itself.

No heroism here, no poet even. The forces of industry, politics, economics and society converge to render a scene of desolation. We see faces and not people; whether their destinies lead, "north or south" there is "no difference". Like a horse rider learning from the horse he is riding, Nasser here begins the poem with his fists tightly gripping the reins, but as the poem progresses, he realizes that he needs to let his world speak itself in order to justify why he will not "defile" his "face by feigning optimism". All he needed to do, and it is no easy task for any poet, is to show us this world, and in a sense, to exit the poem and let it gather itself from the elements he has brought into sharp focus.

IV

This focus on the image is perhaps the first evolution in Nasser's practice and marks the stamp of his generation of poets. Nasser's objective verse and cinematic, documentary patience are on full exhibit in much of his earlier work in poems such as "Textile Workers," "Praise for Another Café," "Concrete," and "One Flower." Characters are given to us through their own words, appearance, and movements. An atmosphere of foggy aspirations contends with trenchant despair, and the desire to flee often surrenders to the pull of warm and comforting companionship that has anchored one's life so far.

With this skill at objective description in hand, Nasser seizes on the central fact of his existence up to then:

even before the poet had left his native Jordan he senses that a long exile has begun. In his second, third, and fourth books, *Climbing the Mountain Since Gilead, Shepherds of Solitude*, and *The Strangers Arrive*, Nasser probes the landscape of exile and accounts for its stages. In these books the poet begins by attempting to recover memories and assess his past. This is part of the process of exile. Having been displaced, we sometimes see the past as unreal, as if it had never happened. We also wonder about it usefulness. Nasser, now a bona-fide exile writing his second book of poems, begins to sift through his memories and his cultural inheritance.

The poem titled "Grandfather" is about a larger-than-life figure "whose life cannot be priced/ whose age cannot be measured". This old man refuses to die though "his friends are coughing comfortably/ in spacious graves". He built stables full of horses and raided other tribes; he had raised a family and "his grandchildren escaped work in the wheat fields,/ escaped floods and wars./They have settled their own regions with women and clans." The old man is a metonym for Nasser's inheritance that refuses to die. Time and recollection drive the poet to look deeper into this inheritance and his probing leads him to question it. "Fathers/ told us about raids/ and deaths avenged,/ but they never told us about martyrs" writes the poet about what was suppressed. All that mattered to the fathers was the ringing of bells around their goats' throats that tinkled their measure of wealth. They also treasured the horses they rode through grazing lands. These two iconic images of his people do not suffice the poet, especially since they ignore the costs that such a heroic life must have incurred. "Night and horses – is this what history is all about?" asks the poet.

Eventually the poet learns what that history entailed. Addressing howdahs, the canopied, decorated seats placed on the backs of camels, the poet cries out:

Howdahs!
Howdahs!
from here my people passed
naked and thirsty
dragging behind them
a dried-up river
and ancient, dying hawks.

Beyond the heroism and struggle, beyond the beauty of the landscape, the exoticism, and the erotic draw of the howdah, this is what life on the deserts of the Arabian peninsula entailed. Nasser's revelation about the past echoes what V S Naipaul called "undated time" and "historical darkness" where even recent events are placed into the realm of legend. Of course, what actually remained in people's memories is what managed to escape their collective repression. In the short poem quoted above, Nasser demonstrates that he can see through the legends of the fathers. Furthermore, he vows in the poem "Lampoon" that he "will not fantasize about the Arabs' great conquests/. . . that Paris is a stable for our horses". Now "broken-hearted like a falcon,/ uprooted like a storm" the poet declares that he will never forget the "hunger on desert plains" in order to sustain an appreciation for his region's history that is based on reality rather than legend.

In his third and fourth books Nasser turns his gaze to the turmoil of exile as he and his friends experienced it. As well as chronicling the existential implications of exile, *Shepherds of Solitude* should also be noted for the effort that the poet takes to create a community. "Can't you see? We haven't changed much," he writes addressing his friends. Exile, we learn, can stunt a person's ability to change and adapt. Nasser here is not talking about himself alone; he is addressing his fellow exiles speaking most of the poems in this book in the first-person plural. These fellow exiles share a sense of nostalgia ("O how lustrous/ and flamboyant/ women used to be"), as well as a sense of eroding agency ("We trembled/ a great trembling/ but the words/ were unmoved"). There is a great deal of loneliness, and apprehension caused by the fluctuations in their lives. There are frequent thoughts of suicide.

The Strangers Arrive expands this examination of exile into the subconscious manifestation of displacement and probes the imaginative compensations that take place in the process. The poet speaker's sense of time begins to slip away. "I arrived with the others,/ slightly before them,/ and after they spread their tools on the ground," he writes. Which one is it, we may ask, with them, before them, or after them? We do not get an answer for we are now dealing with another historical darkness, or the exile's conscious effort to access timelessness and exist beyond the contingencies of his age. The strangers of the book's title are from a historical future or a futuristic past full of princes, biblical scenes, brigands, holy men, political assassinations, and intrigue. The poems in this volume are akin to a dream diary of the speaker of the poem "Once Upon a Time on an Island" who tells us, "I spent my time's gold/ in beds weighed down with insomnia."

V

Disorienting as solitude may be, it does have its pleasures and revelations. In the volume, *Joy to All Who See You*, Nasser shifts gears dramatically and explores the joys of intimacy rather than the desolation of exile. Here the poet devotes his attention to love and the pleasures of the body. He chants his invocations and sings his praise of his beloved by naming her parts, seemingly touching them with the light of his insatiable gaze:

Show it to me
just aroused from sleep
bloated with promise,
dew on its crown,
pomegranate seeds
adoring its ears.

★

I want
to see
it
out of its
hiding,
pulling
toward it
all the morning's
dew.

These lines are as delicate as they are bold. We can guess what the "it" refers to in these passages and realize that the speaker's desire is at its peak. Some of Nasser's earlier poems such as "Viva" and "Shepherds of Solitude" examine the theme of love, mostly of the lost and unrequited variety. Here we encounter a different energy. The speaker's covetousness and erotic appetite are unshakeable. Moreover, this new fire has a refinement about it. We are no longer in the world of howling wolves and haggard falcons, but are presented with images of morning dew and pomegranate seeds adorning a pair of earlobes.

Nasser's visit to Andalusia in the early 1990's immersed him deeper into the world of refinement and returned him to his ongoing meditation on exile. The inspiration for the volume, *Ascent of Breath*, is the life of Abu Abdallah Muhammad Al-Saghir, the last Arab prince of Granada whose ousting in 1492 brought Arab and Muslim presence in the Iberian peninsula to an end. Remembered by many artists since then, Al-Saghir's grief, symbolized as the Moor's last sigh, still evokes a collective, aggrieved sigh among all Arabs. Andalusia was the site of Arab civilization's pinnacle. Not only is Andalusia a paradise lost, but like childhood or innocence, a paradise unrecoverable.

As other artists before him had done, Nasser responded to Al-Saghir's tragic allure. A cultured man, Al-Saghir knew the measure of his loss, but it nonetheless stunned him. Here's how Al-Saghir speaks his grief:

> Did I see, or was it what fever projected?
> Longings waved their lanterns
> at people crossing the dark nights of their souls
> and who would never reach their beds.
> I saw forgiveness hosting brigands who fled the
>   remains of their names.
> I saw brotherhood spread between two giants who

horrified the realms,
clouds shade an orphan abandoned by his kin,
and the treasure guarded by seven ghosts reveal
 itself.
On that loose evening a dying hope held by your
 captive
retrieved its vigor
when your hand
ascended
and touched
my hand,
and I began to see.

In Nasser's rendering above, Al-Shaghir resides in both Dante's inferno and paradiso. This fabulous vision in the first stanza anthropomorphizes human attributes and establishes a new order of things. In the second stanza a tender erotic exchange takes place and that's when the human world does indeed come to the fore. This interaction between the unfathomable forces of the world and our choices as flesh-bound human beings is what draws Nasser to Al-Saghir. His legend offers the poet a cosmic backdrop on which to illustrate the state of the soul in the no-man's land of exile.

The last collection of his work taken for these selections accomplishes two contrary aims. Titled *Life Like A Broken Narrative*, this volume of prose poems attempts to gather as much of that broken narrative as possible. As in a family reunion, all the aspects that the poet had addressed in his previous poetry come together to line up in solidarity to fortify the poet's life and also to compete for his favour. The poet goes back home to his parents' house, visits people who had a deep impact on him, and travels to sites that impressed him in childhood. He confronts his romantic victories and failures. He meditates on his life in exile where he has discovered the pleasures of domesticity. The past is readily at hand and the friends of early manhood still provide companionship as he settles into middle age.

This collage of the various facets his life shows Nasser as a masterful narrator and shaper of wonderful parallels. His neighbour Mrs Morrison, a stodgy middle-class English woman, turns out to be much like his own grandmother. A young ingrate ignoring his lover's solicitations reminds the poet of his own squandering of past love. Things change: The old radio is tossed in a storage room left to fend for itself among other discarded things. Things remain the same: the poet's sisters still keep time in the family household by the different kinds of tea they make. A vision he saw in childhood dogs the poet and refuses to let go of him. The poet knows that his quest for an answer to his vision is utter folly. Nasser manages this balancing act among his ambivalences with the aid of a radical transformation of his poetic practice. Dedicated to verse, he now gives us a whole book of prose poems, and shunning his command of the poetic line – from short to long – he focuses on the sentence. Impossible at times to replicate in English, Nasser's sentences are sinuous and rangy. He experiments with the Arabic sentence, stretching its clauses and heaping modifiers upon it, only to see how much load it can take. In his last volume Nasser comes close to bringing many issues to a close, and he does it by busting open his poetic endeavour.

VI

Through these progressive formal and thematic transformations in a volatile quest for self-understanding, Nasser's poetry nonetheless displays some recurring concerns. The Bedouin heritage is his ancestors' gift of to him. In most of his books the poet reminds us of this inheritance and we see him struggle with it, assessing its merits and bearing its burden. His heritage emphasizes a heroism that seems the stuff of fables more than reality. The poet decides this is not for him:

> I want to cast off from my body
> the shirts of war and peace
> and wipe away the dust of opposing conquests.
> I want to walk alone
> and shut the stable door behind.

We are fortunate in English for this accidental double meaning of the word "stable". Stability is what the tired, worn-out, exiled poet wants. He wishes to put an end to his travels that seem to link him too closely to his ancestors who had roved over the parched plains of his country.

Still, Nasser also finds in the roving Bedouin an ideal heroic figure. In his most eloquent poem addressing Bedouin life, "Shepherds of Solitude", Nasser acknowledges the pull of sedentary life as well as the hardship of nomadic existence that he describes in detail. As much as he tries to convey the hardship, the poet repeatedly veers toward celebration of that life. Listen to these lines:

> He bears the tattoo of his lineage
> inherited for eternity to be carried into epochs of fire.
> He holds the blade of revenge and the mirror of revelation.
> In the midst of rapture he talks
> with a woman who lifted her dress above her knees
> and tread a river of ringing bells.
> In a wilderness that blood cannot reach until it is greened like death,
> where imagination is in drought
> and ancient prophecy is in its eternal spring
> and where commandments chew on sticks to clean

their teeth,
he flowed like a liquid on the paths
and hissed with the snakes.
He wove a road through the Milky Way
with a thread of goat hair
and befriended a wolf and ran alongside him
on feet made of boxthorn.
He let down his hair for a young eagle
who'd lost its way, but was guided to him.
Behind the fence of his soul
lions roared, eager for the pounce
and the cracking of bones.
A cage in his chest,
a leap from the horse of his heart,
a cry in his throat
that would slay a bird of prey . . .

What life could be more heroic? Why would one shun the dignified connection with nature and this indomitable will to survive? It is a painful life, but full of glory and self-realization. Nothing in the domesticated world can evoke such powerful interactions.

What is haunting Nasser in this poem is not merely social or cultural, but also literary. In the lines above we hear echoes of the great sa'luk poets of pre-Islamic Arabia, specifically Shanfara and Ta-abbata Sharran. The sa'luks were brigands who survived in bands or alone and who raided tribal settlements in gangs or stealthily burgled them. They had a thieves' code of honour among themselves and no moral code whatsoever when dealing with those they raided or stole from. They had become brigands because of racism (many were black) and poverty, and most never wished to rejoin society.

The sa'luks had too much blood on their hands to be forgiven. The sole reason the Arab world still celebrates them is their poetry. The most famous qassida of the poet Shanfara has some of the best descriptions of desert life, its hunger and hardship, its skies and wide expanses, its wildlife and the potential for kinship between man and beast. The sa'luks were indeed shepherds of solitude whose crimes are almost forgiven by the genius of their poetic gifts. They provide a fascinating model for an exiled poet seeking freedom and inspiration by breaking rules. Part of Nasser's inheritance, the sa'luks spirit of rebellion and lyrical gifts echoes throughout his poetry.

VII

From his first ventures to woo a young woman away from a more deserving friend in the poem "Viva" to his tale of jealousy in "Something Like Anger, Like Betrayal", Nasser's poetry has consistently engaged in an examination of the masculine. What is a man, how must he behave before men, before women? What should a man value in himself, in women, in other men and in the world? In "Viva" we see two approaches: One is that of the speaker of the poem and the other is his friend's. Both are attracted to a beautiful woman, but clearly the poet's friend comes out as more sympathetic. It's his gift of words and art and even his shyness that we find sympathetic in him. In the process the poet speaker discovers a different dimension of the masculine and the potential for compassion to be found there. The poems in Nasser's last book are chock full of such revelations. In "A Resemblance" the speaker sees a version of himself in someone in a bar ranting against women and raging at his luckless love life. The speaker cringes at the resemblance between him and the man he's watching. In "Puppy Dog" a young man that reminds him of how he had squandered the affections of the young women who clearly loved him. The speaker can barely hold himself from grabbing the ingrate young man by the collar and telling him the facts of life, or how to be a man.

Furthermore, several women emerge as fascinating interlocutors for the poet. In some cases we see the poet speaker trying to capture his beloved in the net of his praise, attempting to contain her. In the volume *Joy to All Who See You* the poet's efforts prove rather taxing. He needs more than one invocation to bring blessings upon his beloved. In the first attempt at naming her in "A Rose of Black Lace," he is blinded by the purity of her beauty represented by the colour white, or blinded perhaps by the contrast between her "black" and her "white". He goes on to make a litany, or another invocation, of her alluring aspects: "White/ with a birth mark,/ with marble,/ the white of sapphire,/ the white of her turn . . ." The second invocation gives us a similar incantation of her beautiful parts. The concluding poem in the volume also launches into a song of praise:

You,
your name,
the ring of your voice
your kiss
your saliva
your summit and plain . . .

This adamic act of naming represents the poet's wish to claim his beloved. The repetition of this naming ceremony, however, suggests that he may never be able to stop being a supplicant to her. During the act of naming, the namer temporarily surrenders to the object he is attempting to name. It is the price he must pay so he can possess her. In this book, the beloved's female body continues to demand more names from the poet and makes the act of naming endless. The poet becomes eternally devoted without ever controlling her. His attempt to contain her within language ends up causing him to speak endlessly, revealing to him the insufficiency of his language.

In rendering the anguish of Mohammad Al-Saghir in *Ascent of Breath*, Nasser presents a "young envied maiden" who dominates the first poem. Nasser lets her range freely unassailed by the intrigue surrounding her. Her erotic prowess allows her to become a source of strength amidst much destruction and enfeeblement. Also, the women in *Life Like A Broken Narrative* are powerfully present. Instead of naming, the poet is listening to women here. The image of the disapproving mother expressed throughout his work ceases to cause the poet grief when we reach the poem "A Dog's Tale." With a measure of irony, the poet recognizes some truth in her assessment of him. To define and understand the masculine, the poet suggests, we must turn to women for the answers.

VIII

Nasser's lyrical gifts are undeniable as I am certain the reader will recognize. Whether working in an objective, documentary mode such as in "Textile Workers" or when roving the complex psychic architecture of Arab Granada, his gift for detail allows him to let the image do the work. Nasser is also gifted with the ability to infuse the magical into everything he describes. "The factories' engines spin/ in the sway of morning jasmine . . ." he writes offering a fascinating parallel, physically impossible, but artistically pleasing. I think one of Nasser's greatest gifts is his unwavering gaze at his own life and experience. Raised in an atmosphere were heroism was demanded, Nasser, in his poetry, manages to free himself from self-justification and to offer us instead a poetry committed to self-examination. In poems such as "Fatigue," "Bent Branches", "Once Upon a Time On An Island", "Ascent of Breath", and in much of *Life Like A Broken Narrative*, Nasser is like a shepherd watching over a flock of wayward, reckless versions of himself. He gives these selves free rein to act out their crises and victories, and they in turn reveal to him various shades of the glory and folly of human nature. Their flaws recounted and noted, he shepherds them home at the end of the day and closes the stable door behind him.

Khaled Mattawa
Ann Arbor,
31 January 2009

from *Praise for Another Café*, 1979

GATES TO THE SKY, BUT
THEY ARE NARROW

I
I will not defile my face feigning optimism.
I will spread the plank of my chest for the birds
coming from the desert and the sea, and I will exhale
a bundle of living smoke. Then I will stop speaking.

II
The heart was stubborn,
a boy with reckless hair
stumbling through night's dilapidated branches.
The city had not yet become
a losing bet.
They usually shot hot lead between the eyes of
the horse that lost. My cramped fingers
did not obey me,
but reached for a net that held emptiness
or a grave that held no corpse.
I touched a hand made of pliable steel.
I did not fire.

The city was drowning
in the sound of neighing.

III
Where does sadness go,
where do cigarettes,
if the cafés disappear?
The small poets,
their foam,
their impartial criticism,
and their stories, suitable only
for diaries of wretchedness . . .
Where will you build your fabled kingdom, dear
  dream?
. . . .
. . . .
Cafés are more rooted here
than fingernails are in fingers.
So what is the harm in this?

IV
The heart is a morsel of rare sponge.
It cannot shield itself from tremors
coming at it from all directions.
The city could not raise its keen sword.
Despair was the widest of the sky's narrow gates.

V
I will not defile my face feigning optimism
to please the wife and the seven neighbours.
Sadness, the horse most likely to win,
met me on the road
and offered his dark, veined hand to me.
I offered out my hand too
and we laughed together:
The city's night is long
without those celestial bodies
made of phosphate and human flesh.
And though they are pavilions
of bad poetry and impartial criticism
of the fog of endless cigarettes,
the cafés are low stones,
rest houses
for birds coming from the desert
or from the sea.

VI
Amman smells of horses
and of the lone shirt hung
in the widow's wardrobe.
Amman smells like tired bodies.
I recall:
*Was the Arab Bank
close to where the river shrank,*

close to dawn's first spark?
Was it far from my heart?
They begin to tremble those fingers pointing to the sky.
No . . .
It was a summer whose fires would not go out,
a time of collapse.

VII
In seconds, the scene takes shape:
leather bags of different sizes
and different contents,
faces that go long
and cloud up,
features that take the shape of cramped muscles.
The train heads north or south.
No difference.
The long whistles
become a thin, agitated
thread.
And the scene folds upon itself.

Cities more distant than this dream,
this whistling
will never reach you!

TEXTILE WORKERS

The factories' engines spin
in the sway of morning jasmine,
in flesh,
through the road, two arm-spans wide,
curving out
from the dark trees.
The factories' engines spin
in the early buses that carry
the workers to a factory in the suburbs
near Marka.
They spin
(they lit their fires
in the city's ash)
circled by thin smoke:
A worker,
two workers,
fifty
drift past
like copper butterflies,
like heavy iron.

I
They know the threads and what their colours
   suggest:

Blue for curtains, sex, and rooms in tall towers . . .
Green for carpets and the university campus . . .
Red, ----------------
White, for shrouds.
They know
their syndicate,
stone
by stone,
their arms,
arm
by arm,
and the road to their desolate restaurant.

II
A worker,
two,
fifty,
walk to the end of the sun
on the long sidewalk.
They head toward
a restaurant near "the Central",
a restaurant that knows these long faces
the way the shadows know the cane chairs.
They eat their chickpeas in the afternoon.
Then the curve of their street leads them
to women,
to a wide commotion.

PRAISE FOR ANOTHER CAFÉ

Another Café
You may,
you who have never stopped betting,
you may leave now:
no direction,
no suitcases,
no water in your time's jug,
no wife in clean clothes,
no rain in the gutters,
no star in the sky that breaks your back
since your contentment diminished.
Am I not right?
Isn't it one coffin and you'll never have to worry
 again!
– *Have you been here long?*
The Island Café did not fall to its knees
that evening.
It had no wish to be on another street,
and did not find its building too small,
or feel shame for the meager warmth
supplied by a wood-burning stove.
The café was not fed up with its perennial customers
and felt no need to hire attractive women
from coastal cities.

It never felt like a heavy guest,
like your very own hands.
It did not spread like blood.
– *And what do you say?*
– *I'm hoping to stumble upon a morning*
that suits my rhythm
and the valley's insects.

Another Morning
Every morning
he surprised us with the possibility of travel
to other cities,
with the same rectangular face
and those pimples –
acne that he called "an affliction of the young" –
the same expressions
and the dangling cigarette.
– *Are you leaving?*
– *This morning is as good as any.*
– If you wish it could …
Then he looks toward the vanishing horizon,
those distant clouds above the invisible mountain
  paths,
then another look at the tea served at the Island Café,
the warmth he felt when touching the glass cup,
and a third look to the companions around him,
their daily kinship in language he understands.

The bird of tragedy falls into his waning blood,
and he cannot find his way
to the beginning.

Another Talk
That wasn't his only wish, and he never had any luck
with happiness. His body, burning with dreams
(quickly extinguished in cold asphalt) continued
  singing
a song preordained in its tragedy and yearning.
He besieged us with maps,
with possibilities, and an empty gaze.
He always wanted to see surprise in our faces,
and wanted home among the nations.
He searched among his fingers for the burn of exile
and among his socks for the body of a woman.
He did not seek a language
that would retrieve lost time
or reward him with poetry
long after his steps and suitcases
had gone their separate ways.
And he did not . . .
and he was not . . .
All countries are a stone's throw away
but the country his hand could not reach
remained unpeopled to him, and empty of stones.

Can a poem begin with "I"
and not end in desiccation?
What wind has not aimed for my skull?
It wasn't the wish to walk into fog
or rain falling from eyes.
It was this bouncing body
that carried me to song or suicide.

Another Alibi
In the snows of Gilead there is no difference between
thick coats and flowered shirts
blossoming with the blood of Ashrafiya.
These awful pimples remain on your rectangular face
and the Island Café remains in the King Faissal
   district,
and God remains in the midst of departure,
and you remain without a wife in your clothes.

And there's no star
in the sky
to break
your back
now
that your contentment
has diminished.

VIVA

I

The sun opens her lilac hands
behind Viva's house,
her house
between two houses,
between a horse made of winter wood
and a café where the little poets drink their tea
and feel proud of all the cigarettes they smoked
and the last poems they wrote.
Viva and the earth begin together
toward the sky whose colour resembles
the clouds' and the clouds are a book of grass.

Viva leaves her house in the morning.
Jasmine surprises her
and the smell of tea,
and the workers of the Bata factory.
When we meet at the Marka bus station,
she says as she searches her pocket,
– *Want to meet again tonight?*
Then she tucks a paper airplane in my pocket.
– *I'll be at the union office,*
she says.

Shepherd of Solitude

II
My friend meets her at a traffic light
and searches in her face for words
for his next poem.
He widens his eyes, taken by
the supple lines of her figure.
(He would have died to become a sculptor,
but his hands were too small).

. . . .
. . . .

She'll go with him to an event
at the women's union,
and he'll feel ashamed of his dirty jacket.

. . . .
. . . .

Then she asks him,
Where is the Lady of Ashrafiya?
He feels shy again like a water lily
and begins to talk about the language of stone,
about Michelangelo,
and birds circling the window
picking drops of dew from young women's hair.

III
. . . and I know two eyes
calm
and ferocious . . .

If he tries to speak of poetry
or if he tries to dance
or if he tries to speak of stones,
Viva extends a hand to him
and he smiles, confused,
then takes the jasmine blossom from her fingers.
She tells him about a trip to the South
and about Shafei who seduced all the Earth's birds
and who built trees for those coming from the ends
   of the world
who fled
while the cities looked away . . .

IV
My friend begins to sing to her:
   No gold,
   O Lady of Ashrafiya,
   can buy
   your high-browed mane.
   No gold can afford
   your face, round
   and full like a moon.
   The bright stars
   shine suspended
   trembling in your eyes
   They shape a bridge
   of poplar wood

that stretches from
your love of poetry
to the sea, a road
dotted with orange trees . . .
Then he sees me
(I'm buying tobacco).
Silence muffles him
little
by little
and he slinks away
not wishing for a crisis between us,
leaving Viva and me
with a language of stone
that we speak with our hard cast
fingers.

CONCRETE

Feet lead us
to brief states of darkness,
and we dare not go further.
This usually happens in large buildings,
in shelters.
We climb the stacked, inert
stone steps.
We light a match
(if we had any love for tobacco),
reach out our hands,
and they strike a cold surface,
solid sheets of cement.
Flakes of whitewash and rheumatism shower upon us.
We climb other walls
and reach out our hands again,
but there's no wood to satiate our need for company,
no underwear.
We light our cigarettes
to shake with living smoke
the hegemony of cement.
And to affirm our instinctive and mannered courage,
we release a tune as a plea for rescue.
The doors are made of solid steel.
Locks like scorpions from Asian steppes
throb on the doors.

Shepherd of Solitude

Where will these feet take us
when they're only made of ten toes?
They are our feet's hoarse bells
climbing the concrete steps
with a mixture of vine fibre,
fear,
and a little blood.
No way to deny them, these feet,
low-bound lumps
swimming in prairies of cement.

A SONG AND THREE QUESTIONS

I
Talk is silver,
poetry is gold,
and women are the ringing of both metals.
Poems
will be our songs from now on.
Let's start without allusions or embellishments
and look at the living things between us
with an eye for praise.
Let our words
celebrate our contentedness
and those joys known only to shepherds.
Their songs spread along
with the smell of their armpits
among goat paths and scrub grass,
and they have disappeared never to return.

II
Shall we blow into a silver trumpet?
But how can shepherds live without songs
or sheep
or desires?
No, we'll sing.
How could there be shepherds without horses and

violins
and wounds that never heal?

III
Talk is silver,
poetry gold,
and women are the ringing of both metals.
Poems will be our songs from now on.
Let's dedicate them
to those who will never return,
to the shepherds of hazy dawns,
to the chants dressed in wedding clothes,
to the women who loved the fiercest stags
and who preferred the Eros of copper,
spring grasses and buried wells,
falcons and night predators and the tigers of Arabia,
cymbals, bayonets, skiffs and saddles,
studded with the blood of the tribes,
the shouts of boys yet to learn how to
tame their mares,
and the flight of whole tribes from open country
pulling hard at iron bits.

Broken flutes
and hollow bones
will surprise us with three questions:
How much time has passed?

Have the old wounds healed?
What names are still in use?
How do we answer?
Will it be enough to say,
talk is silver, poetry gold
and women are the ringing of both metals
and poetry will be our language from now on?

Fellow shepherds, let's dig
into our bowls filled to the brim.
Let us begin our chants.

from *Climbing the Mountain Since Gilead*, 1981

SONG

Blood in school books,
blood in the first note
of the royal anthem,
blood in the military academies,
blood climbing the minarets.
Even on the arc of the crescent moon there's blood.
On the slopes of the seven mountains, blood.
Blood between the trees and their bark,
between our lips and our song of praise.

PLACES

From those places that banished us
to the boredom of lives
lived in suitcases
we keep pictures
of family.
Pictures with shifting colours
of a family glowing with
tribal pride,
ennui of travel,
and a postal service that does not work:
This is all that has remained
of our mothers.

Amjad Nasser

EXCERPTS FROM THE BODY'S SURA

I
They will have silver
circling their wrists.
They will have
curves
and details,
and limber muscles.
Their loose hair
will be drenched on brief evenings
with the psalm of joy.

II
The moons of desire
tremble on the young men's bodies.
Then they wilt and lose their light.
And where the wings of night birds
flutter,
a song
pricks the reeds of their souls
from ten different directions.

III
Body, stop your endless

wrestling with the wind,
with iron
and all sordid beasts.

IV
They will have bees
rising from the armpits' nectar.
They'll have the breasts' roundness
and the fingers' light touch.
They will not dream of other things
while here.
They will read verses from their book
and toss their heads back.

LAMPOON

Like a broken-hearted falcon,
like a toothless storm,
I will lean on the edge of the city
and block with my back
the arrows that friends fling at me.
I will remember my grandmother's long pipe
and I will not fantasize about the Arabs' great
   conquests
and I will not think that Paris is a stable for our
   horses
and I will not weep over the Pyrenees
as they melt in your hands like a block of ice
and I will not roll the sleeves of my caftan
toward God to honour Al-Ghafiqi[1].
When the parade of the kings of Banu Ahmar[2]
floats past my feet,
I will not force my eyelids to return a greeting.
I will remember the sword and the leather rug.

---

1 Abdulrahman Al-Ghafiqi (d. 732) led the Andalusian Muslims into battle against the forces of Charles Martel in the Battle of Tours on October 10, 732 AD for which he is primarily remembered in the West. With the defeat of his army the Arab advance on Europe was checked.
2 Banu Ahmar were the last Muslim dynasty in Adalusia. Expelled in 1492, their domain by then was largely restricted to the city of Granada.

Shepherd of Solitude

I will remember the bribes of gold and silver.
I will remember hunger on desert plains.
I will remember the brigands and stags
that came to drink from my wounded palm.
All this while I lean on the edge of the city
broken-hearted like a falcon,
uprooted like a storm.

Amjad Nasser

GRANDFATHER

What is this old man waiting for
now that his friends are coughing comfortably
in spacious graves?
The trees that witnessed his youthful strength
now have withered beards and stooped backs.
His stables, built out of holly-oak wood,
have crumbled into dust that has dissolved
in water that never stops preaching its sermons.
What is this old man waiting for, this old man
whose life cannot be priced,
whose age cannot be measured
by the houses he built or the ones that collapsed,
or the horses that died in regions God made and forgot,
and that are now relieved of his unbearable weight?
His grandchildren escaped work in the wheat fields,
escaped floods and wars.
They have settled their own regions with women and
   clans.
They have ruined cities with rebellions, and tied laurel
   branches
and bullet belts around their waists and chests.
They took horses and tobacco to regions untouched
except by the hooves of wild goats.
They built forts, brought dead soil to life,
and spread through the land.

WINGS

The things of those who departed
went on gleaming in the yard.
What traveller could avoid
their mysterious magic?
And those who stayed,
how could they forget
the joy they felt staring
at those strong faces
spread on living marble?
They left us
and their things continued
to pierce our souls
like small birds.

FATIGUE

I am tired of my shirt
and my hands and my neighbours
who never stop fucking and fighting,
and who, when we meet in the hall,
smile with all their teeth so that I have to
pretend to be present in their presence.
I am tired of the letters I wait for.
Who will write them? Which stamps
will bring more happiness?
I am tired of the country that gnaws
at my flesh and tracks me down with boredom,
tired of the clothes suicides left behind.
I am tired of Tayseer Subul's poems
and the others who go on publishing
their wretched books.

ONE FLOWER

Flowers in the hair of the woman going
to a dance.
There is music, kisses and gold rings
inside the woman's body.
Flowers on the balconies facing a blacksmith's shop.
It's a simple evening:
artisans and retired workers,
lovers unemployed by love,
grocers,
the same evening facing
all the balconies.
Flowers in the room of the novelist who has a deer
 fetish,
deer and murdered revolutionaries in the novelist's
 room.
Flowers, deer, and a novelist in a single room.
Flowers in colourful clay pots.
Roof tiles on houses inhabited
by the acids of happiness.
Flowers and sex and rumpled silk stockings
in the rooms of the university dorm.
University girls and wine.
Birth control pills in their apartments,
the university boys deeply engaged with women and
 rallies.

Flowers in the poets' poems,
lice in the poets' hair,
and the poets loaf about without flowers or poems.
A carnation in the old politician's lapel.
The old politician removes the flower
to protest the war.
The war does not end.
The flowers of the four seasons
are in the garden of the bourgeois divorcée
who drives
along the sea shore
every evening.
She is looking for a hole
in the wall of man.
Many flowers,
and one flower for me,
which
a stranger
tosses
through
my window
thinking
his old
lover
still
lives
here.

SHIRTS

This is a shirt.
A little old, and billowy,
and in need of a woman's touch, say.
It's a bit tattered at the collar,
a little dark in the armpits,
but one can still wear it for a walk
or while leading a flock of goats
through unsteady winds.

★

Don't go far, dear friend.
The shirt has nothing to do with the man
whose statue stands in the square
alone like a god of boredom.
Don't let your fancy lead your far.
This shirt has been honoured by defeat,
but it has nothing to do with that man.

★

It's a shirt.

★

When we start our mornings
wearing flowery shirts
we have to give a great, wide greeting

to the coming day.

★

Each morning we wake up with our assassinated
 dreams,
the taste of night's acids on our lips.
And on our lips there are defeated wishes and the
 remains of words.
We hurry to drawers and clothes lines
and with wild motions
we spill the dried clothes
seeking the most suitable shirt.

★

What wind can dry these shirts
that have drowned in pleasure?

★

Farmers plant long-fibre cotton
but run about wearing scales.

★

When bullets are shot at us
from hidden outposts and when lead penetrates our
 shirts
a whistling begins, indicating blood.
And when flowers are aimed at us from orchards
and when hands that had almost fallen asleep

begin to glow with a light that resembles the feel of
 kisses . . .

★

At night shirts fall on their faces
seeking fallen stars
and dropped buttons.

★

If they ask you about shirts,
say
they are the body's flag
and desire's sail.

THE BLEATING OF COPPER

Fathers
told us about raids
and deaths avenged,
but they never told us about martyrs.
The bells of the flock
were everything;
the bleating of copper
that never ceased its ringing.
And the rivers and oases
that slipped from under
the hooves of their horses at night!
Night and horses –
is this what history is all about?

TO YOU, HOWDAHS !

Howdahs!
Howdahs!
bells of the desert,
from here the Jordanians passed
swordless, barefoot,
in their souls
solid boulders rubbed against each other
and from their dusty beards
rose the sounds of howling wolves.
Howdahs!
Howdahs!
from here my people passed
naked and thirsty
dragging behind them
a dried-up river
and ancient, dying hawks.

from *Shepherds of Solitude*, 1986

EXILE

Can't you see?
We haven't changed much.
Maybe we haven't changed at all:
The loaded statements,
the Bedouin accent,
the long embrace,
the questions about family and livestock,
the ringing laugh,
the smell of old wood
(wood stored in stables)
still lingering on our clothes.
Can't you see?
We haven't changed much,
maybe not at all.
We squat and jabber,
while jumbled laundry hangs on clothes lines
in front of our houses,
and children covered with grime.
Mint tea in the evening,
lively gossip,
contentment with little,
and obsession with revenge,
the blood thicker than water –
all this
as if we're still in Mafraq or Salt,

in Kerak or Ramtha,
as if we never crossed northern borders
to the big cities
and coastlines
where wars rage
and seas surge.

Here strangers grab each other
by the collar
or fire their guns
from balconies
into each other's clothes lines.

OVERDUE CONVERSATION

Our old words
were said without mercy.
All the mischief we wanted to make,
others now openly commit
without a hint of shame.
The words
that made our heads spin
in years spent running
away from family
are oxidized in the brain.

I
O God,
how luminous those
words were,
how flamboyant,
like mares
under the whip.

II
The women
we dreamt of
as we bit the edges

of our weary moustaches,
and as we tore
the quiet of night
like knives –
the city's thieves have raped them
while standing upright
in air-conditioned offices,
their curtains wide open,
facing the street.

III
Mohammad,
O how lustrous
and flamboyant
women used to be,
like wild mares
dressed in
gilded saddles!

IV
In our old words
"the people" rode
each other's shoulders
and shouted for freedom.
In our words in that era
a prince was still a prince,

Shepherd of Solitude

bearded and anointed
with perfumes,
and "the people"
used to tremble
when the chord of words
was struck.

VI
We trembled
a great trembling,
but the words
were unmoved.

Amjad Nasser

BENT BRANCHES

I want to purge my soul
of all signs of obedience
and the last clots of forgiveness.
I want to cleanse my face
and wipe away the tribe's features,
cut off the branches of the family tree.
I want to erase poetry's rot
and the futility of remembrance.
I no longer wish for grey, hazy dusks
or to stand under an array of spectral lights.
I want
only
to hear the tremor of the world
beating against my heart's walls,
to see
light
dissolve
in the swampy waters of my eyes.
I want to clear my head
of all that remains of sermons and the good word.
I want to purge my heart
of my first love's rubble, its shards of glass.
I want to clear my eyes
of the moon's tattered nets,
curtains that shutter windows close.

Shepherd of Solitude

I want to purge my voice of the acid of song,
of cries wrapped in silver threads.
I want to shake birds' nests off
my shoulders,
those mute morning birds.
I want to cast off from my body
the shirts of war and peace
and wipe away the dust of opposing conquests.
I want to walk alone
and shut the stable door behind me.

Amjad Nasser

LONELINESS

At night
when walls breathe
and the steam rising from concrete
reaches our fingers
and fills our noses,
when
we seek frowned faces
and cracked hands,
when
we shout all our strength
into boxes shut tight,
when
an echo does not return,
when
we raise our hands
and a shadow fails to fall,
when
no one knocks on the door
and no one walks past the window,
when
we do not hear the scratch
of the woodworm in the wardrobe
or the howls of love in adjacent rooms,
when
we rush to desks and drawers

Shepherd of Solitude

and find no family pictures,
when
we look for a revolver,
a knife,
or a rope
and find nothing except the plaster on the wall
cracking in unremitting silence,
when
we search for our names
and do not remember them,
when
all this happens
at night
in a box clamped shut,
what do we do?

FEVER

A sway, a stooping,
a slight movement in the shoulders,
a throat shaking off drunken butterflies,
a foggy picture of kitchen utensils,
a light perfume emanating from the wood.

The woman's silhouette stands behind glass:
a silent dialogue,
a half-hearted wave pulls the ragged clothes
off the body's branches.

Ten fingers extend to raise ten violins
toward the mouth.
A ringing sounds from an anklet, a trembling leg.
Two marble shoulders support the window,
but
somewhere else
someone is playing the violin of suffering,
someone is sending fever in the shape
of a sorrowful whistling.

DAILY OCCURRENCE

There wasn't a time when I came home and
a cloud of lead did not follow me. And every time
I opened the door, my own family surprised me.
I should have been more tolerant of the small troubles
our old neighbour used to make for me.
Others conspired with her and placed jugs
of mountain spring water at the elevator door.
There wasn't a single time in which I sat on a chair or
   a bed
that calcified dolls and satanic thoughts did not
   encircle me.
Tasks and orders fell from the suitcases of businessmen
whose presence here surprised me.
And Yara used to set her traps. She used to slip
thin souls out of the shade trees or the tablecloth.
She forced the cruel children to return
the black cat to the animal shelter.
There wasn't a single time in which I did not have to
fight over the ashtrays with hot-tempered creatures.
Many times I asked a woman specifically
to stop tossing fish heads at my feet.
But the radio kept sending the same instructions
to teach the villages how to resist
the hordes of strangers that encircled them
armed with flutes and colourful feathers.

Amjad Nasser

ONCE UPON AN EVENING IN A CAFÉ

When your thoughts
do not take you far
and you're silent
as you tremble
and gaze
at the trellises of your hands,
when the cart of your daydreams
does not lead you into tunnels
lit with apprehensions
and lightning
as you remain silent
and tremble
gazing at the threads of smoke looping
around your wrist,
when the woman who lets
her scarf fall
through the evening's emptiness
greets you, and you fail to
acknowledge
her greeting, but
remain silent and tremble
as you gaze
at the destinies that unfold, swirling
in your coffee cup,
when the new immigrants pass by

Shepherd of Solitude

arm in arm with their local women
blabbering about time that flees
so soon, and you keep silent
as you tremble and gaze
at the table's
ambiguous wood,
where you don't sit with anyone
and remember war
only
as a horseshoe or a coat
riddled with bullets,
when, upon an evening, in a café
the faces pass by you
like copper clouds
as you listen
to cymbals that ring
in a far-away desert
or sails that snap
in imagined bays,
when the blind singer's record
spins, once upon an evening
in a café and the customers sigh
and you walk out
heading for the axe,
to where it leans
against the tree.

WRONG IMPRESSIONS

Who gave this impression
about our new houses,
we who planted basil around the stone bench
and spread the smell of cinnamon and walked
toward the edges of salt?
Who told them that our life
on the islands is not our life
on the other shore?
My friends, who cavorted with she-wolves
and pretended chivalry,
talked a lot about my new house
to people they befriended
on the streets.
My friends who bowed
to their mothers' commands
even after reaching thirty
stopped people on the street
and told them about my new house.

Who gave this impression about our new clothes,
we who took off embroidered vests
and broad belts braided from snake skins
and now all we wear are scales?
Who told them that our shirts
are not as worn at the sleeves

as they were on that other shore?
My friends, who continued to peep
inside low balconies
even after they passed thirty
sat in cafés and told passers-by
about my new clothes.
My friends who never wrote me
went to our neighbours
and told them about my new clothes.
My friends who continue to expose
their chest hair and biceps
even though they too have passed thirty
went to my mother
and began to tell her
about a life I never lived.

SHEPHERDS OF SOLITUDE

I

Who will describe his transformation
and outline with a Bedouin dagger
the parameters of his wisdom?
Who will write about a boy flung by the forces
onto solid concrete
where no dream grows
that is not crowned with defeat?
Who will say that he entered Amman on a spacious,
limpid morning in the year of the great opening,
the year of the earth's fever, and trembled
before a blonde woman reading the book of
 disputation?
Who will say that he took off his sandals and washed
 his hands
with a secret water, that he left his name and coat
 behind,
then pinned the carnation of eternal refusal directly to
 his chest?
Who will know that on a rainy, low-hung morning
he will look upon things and nothing will reach out to
 him
except an image of two hazy fingers shaking like waves
in his hands?

Shepherd of Solitude

Like a man seeking a kiss
or a duel,
he moves on
with a bloody rose in his chest
and a stone in his fist.
Who will know that his mother wept, not for anything
except that he did not wear the woollen sweater she had not finished
knitting?
Who will know that his father, the old infantry officer,
arched his eyebrows when
his letter reached him?

He banished his younger brothers because the letter did not begin:
"Dear Father, dear treasure,
love without measure . . ."
Have you seen him enter cities
and leave
thin,
and wet like pigeon feathers,
distracted like a prophet,
lonelier than Al-Farazdaq's wolf?[3]
Sword without a handle,
horse without legs,
a bloody rose in his chest,
a half moon on his brow.

Man,
son of the dark woman
crowned with silence and gloom,
son of the good father,
there are four lilies shining through the crystals of brotherhood
around your picture in a wooden frame.
There are four daggers in sheaths made of mint
ready to slit the sacrificial ram's throat on your doorstep.
The Verse of the Throne throbs at the entrance of the house,
a basil pot, a fish mouth for a charm,
and the lemon tree
crestfallen in the evening
between the mother's silence
and the father's firm stride
beside the stone path where
a longing leads the old lover
to the scent of her first embrace.

Man,
son of the haggard woman

---

3 Al-Farazdaq (lump of dough), is Hammam ibn Ghalib Abi Firas, (ca 641- ca 728-730)an Arab poet famous for his Lampoons, especially his poetic exchanges with his rival the poet Jarir (ca 650-ca 728). Al-Farazdaq is considered the best satirist in Classical Arab poetry.

crowned with silence and gloom,
son of the good man,
a cloud leans on your sagging shoulders
and shadows have crawled to where your hand rests.
A wounding rain will fall between
your song and the plains of Moab.
The pole star has taken refuge in your soul's bower
and your lips bite on dying enthusiasm.

Man,
son of the woman crowned
with silence and gloom,
son of the good man,
the floral shirt with which you tempted the soldiers' wives
is now worn by a friend who follows in your steps.
The young widow to whom a star of desire led you
through night dew and the turmoil of youth
committed suicide in the room with the iron door.
Between her navel and breasts, raised like traps,
you wrote with henna:
Your flame is not in fire
but in the heart.
Give me a lock of your hair
and go.
I did not know love
but I knew
how to stand

in the light of the last star
behind a fence made of poplar wood.
Give me a sprig of basil and go.
I'd never known how to kiss
but from my mouth butterflies escaped
and a field song sounded . . .
Give me a shattering kiss and go.
Since the bells that rang
from little lambs' throats,
I have longed for the ringing of the anklet
that gives your left ankle
its golden gleam.
And since childhood
since the time of dispersal
and my one-eyed sleep,
I have dreamt
of what I am dreaming now.
Give me
your hand
so I can sleep.

II

For a short time he lived in clarity.
He is now lost among words
and in the fog that grazes on the shoulders' grass.
He stands accused among meanings,

brittle and soggy like a morsel
fit only for a lazy hoopoe,
like a flower that exudes a scent of despair,
like nothing.
And on those nights
when the family
brushed white dust off
the stone of sleep
and sought powerful visions,
he bent, then dived into solitude.
He let go of a scream
that swayed in its high loneliness
and fell:
Master, you . . .
He bears the tattoo of his lineage
inherited for eternity to be carried into epochs of
   fire.
He holds the blade of revenge and the mirror of
   revelation.
In the midst of rapture he talks
with a woman who lifts her dress above her knees
and treads a river of ringing bells.
In a wilderness that blood cannot reach
until it is greened like death,
where imagination is in drought
and ancient prophecy is in its eternal spring
and where commandments chew on sticks to clean
   their teeth,

he flowed like a liquid on the paths
and hissed with the snakes.
He wove a road through the Milky Way
with a thread of goat hair
and befriended a wolf and ran alongside him
on feet made of boxthorn.
He let down his hair for a young eagle
who'd lost its way, but was guided to him.
Behind the fence of his soul
lions roared, eager for the pounce
and the cracking of bones.
A cage in his chest,
a leap from the horse of his heart,
a cry in his throat
that would slay a bird of prey,
O Master, O . . .

III

Did he know when he sought the footsteps
of the shepherds' wisdom
that the prince who led a cavalcade of lovers and thieves
and entered the tunnel of heroism, left nothing in riotous cities
except a crowned darkness and the remains of trumpet squeals?

Did he know that a false prophecy
shot him out of the thicket of brotherhood,
out of his mother's cape
to the mumblings of concrete and lavender grass
piercing the barracks' tin sheets?
Did he know as he wrote the songs of Moab
that Ammun would stab his heart
with the copper shrapnel of tribes banished
when the new dams were built?
The city's door was studded with spying eyes,
bodies as tall as cypresses,
hearts made of stone.
They took off their shoes
at the door of love,
kissed the prince's hand
adorned with gold,
and planted the ground with reeds.

IV

He had to begin this beginning
and reach the ends of his wits
like a lost beast with a collapsed heart.
Defeat and despair weighed on him
and he was like a wolf eating
the corpse of another wolf
under

a sky
empty
of God.
He had to . . .
He did not reach deep into contentment
or into companionship;
he did not go far into the earth,
not far into the north
where the trees
seek hearths and axes.
He had to begin at this end
and go to this extent
while defeat rang in his throat
like the bell around the largest ram.
He had to
deny his astonishments
and select among them.
He had to leap under the spear of time.
He
had to . . .

What sky is this
that you can't even whistle at
or quarrel with
or swap
curses?
   N
   O

Shepherd of Solitude

H
O
P
E
Sky that stifles stone.
No use.
And stone stands firm in the bareness of creation.
Like an eagle in the chapter of rage
he chews on a morsel of annihilation.

IV

He seeks you
and he does not seek salvation,
the man who went past.
He speaks painfully about loss, then dies.
He searches
among the throng of metals
in the ambush of isolation.
He seeks a description that does not follow the described
and puts it down without ink.
He seeks a lost beast
to whom he will cry:

Friend,
let's live together.
You are a lost prince, dear beast, like me,
seeking an evergreen desert
and shepherds who feed the birds
the meat of their shoulders
and enter
the dominion
of the
seasons.

from *The Strangers Arrive*, 1990

CHANCE

I
I arrived with the others,
slightly before them,
and after they'd spread their tools on the ground
to gauge the distances.
The native helpers named the targets
and measured the angles with precise gazes.
The professionals had the task
of categorizing the facts.
Their assistants' intelligence exceeded prior reports
and this left room for speculation.

II
They settled on street corners.
They built a hangar to receive other escapees.
Among those who arrived
by chance I too won this bounty.
From then on, patience
became
a hard
seed
between
my teeth.

THE STRANGERS ARRIVE

The strangers came from other shores and huddled
in forts that stood high above the postal roads.
He thought of boys who ambushed mailmen in
  alleyways
and forced them to confess the strange sources of their
  stamps.

He thought of public notaries and scribes
who sat on wooden platforms, sending their minions
to the markets to catch farmers and nomads who had
  lost
their way to the circles of justice and relief.

He thought of bureaucrats complaining under ceiling
  fans.
They sat and spun on swivel chairs, as servants plied
  them
with glittering sugar and ginger ale.
In their folders dams collapsed and villages were
  abandoned
as thoughtful tax collectors gazed.

He thought of thieves wearing canvas shoes who robbed
camps abandoned by soldiers who left them to subdue
rebels who disturbed the outlying districts

of a land ruled by a king who was once caught spying
on women stripping hair from their legs
with lumps of caramelized sugar.

He thought of a prince who survived a massacre of his aides.
When he woke he saw a caravan urging a frightened boy to sing
and the boy told them the tale of a night of concubines
and mirrors that gleamed with shining swords.

He thought of a friend who was murdered on a side street
by thugs who wanted to prove that the morning paper
can deny a man's death and that a mother's tears in a distant city
are an invention that need not be heeded.

He thought of a day scented with mint on which a parade
of blind snails slugged toward their demise at the edge of a jungle.
Women there spread their aprons on sofas and fed their children
gruel that neighbours cooked. They held a feast for pilgrims just returned

from performing mysterious rituals in the motherland.

He thought of a general who leaned on his spear for forty years
facing foes who had turned to stone on the plain of his vision.
When they saw birds feeding on his head
his foes resumed their march on the villages.

He thought of a holy man and his companion.
They were soon joined by criminals who humiliated
a village and turned its people vile.
When they saw a boat that belonged to orphans they sank it.
And when his companion stared at him in disbelief,
the holy man answered,
have I
not
told
you
that
you
are not
steadfast
enough
to remain
with
me?

The strangers who sewed day to night
have sprawled among torn curtains and food-stained
 plates.
They helped the natives prolong their insomnia
with archives,
machines,
and maps.
They wiped the morning milk staining their lips
and thought of people who smile
at them when they meet,
and who, as soon as they turn their faces,
begin to beat
and beat their animals
with sticks.

THE IMPENDING HOUR

. . . and when the light of dawn shone, the princes fought
their desire for sleep and slaughtered goats
from the steepest mountains with golden swords ...
This commotion continued in a story that unfolded
before witnesses who had brought vegetables and
    livestock
to the marketplace.

As if in a dream they started to recount that they saw:
Roosters eat their cockscombs.
Screams shatter like glass in hallways
and flow like liquid on marble floors.
Dusty horsemen take off soiled helmets in
    bedchambers
and order servants to speak to them in their native
    tongue.

A buzzing that pierces through cardboard
and pours terror into the hearts of seamstresses.
Birds lure short trees and fasten them to distant
    waters.
Hunch-backed moons swing like fans
over motionless creatures in the hills.
Women in labour cling to a wayward moon.

Dancers cavort with lovers who had just left
their wives' embraces.
A false jingling from
coins that thieves exchange for tins of tobacco.
Clerks gaze at tombstones seeking legal addresses.
Women show drowsy judges
the whip-lash marks on their hips.

Shepherds slaughter a ram before a lover who
 exaggerates his surprise.
Fishermen with anchors and leather belts
spread enormous nets on the rocks
and drink a toast to the pirates of ancient days.
Birds
leave the scene,
taking off from the tops
of the spectators' heads.

And the princes exchanged their bloody
coats for gilded ones,
their shoulders gleaming in the dusk.
They sheathed their elegant swords in the dew
of the tale
and folded them within
the book.

1955

I
Among my peers only I received the gift of exile,
and a woman awarded me a blazer that her five sons
  grew out of
and never wore.
And among those who fell by what they thought
were their strengths
I was the only one given an island.
I abandoned it between raids made by blind pirates
who were a miracle of rage.
Then I was given cities indebted to their suicides
for seasons of tranquilized music.

The towers
and the banks
and the souls tossing about under rain
led me to what my hands wrought.

II
The lesson that later generations have deduced
rests on a premonition that has now become a
  method:
he arrived in the year 1955 and they healed him with
  poverty.

Among his peers he was the only one
guided by a cold light to what his eyes saw.

III
My daughter grew up
and saw in all this nothing worth repeating.

LINES TO JOSEPH

Brother,
my brother,
why did you strike me with the beauty of your eyes,
why did you plague me with false blood
and make me seek the wolf's tale
only to return with your bloodied shirt?
Why did you leave your scent in the shirt
that would fly from the amber of the fields
to rest on our father's face?
You were born under the moon of acceptance
and I under the tower of regret.
You amazed me with your vision –
eleven stars held in your hands –
then left me in the grip of sin.
O Brother,
my brother,
why did you strike me with the beauty of your eyes?

Amjad Nasser

ONCE UPON A TIME ON AN ISLAND

For Mahmoud al-Rimawi

I had time like this:
I did everything possible to avoid facing
the late morning hurdles,
and lingered in my limbs
as they freed themselves from sleep.

The noonday sun knows
how calm my breathing was
as I fell into an avalanche of loneliness.

I had enough time to give the evening
its share of bygone pleasures
and rains that fell
from the depth of memory.

The nights that my guests punished
with swigs of cognac
will bear witness that I cheered
as the torch bearers leapt into a mysterious race.
They will attest that I spent my time's gold
in beds weighed down with insomnia.

from *Joy to All Who See You*, 1994

INVOCATION FOR ENTERING THE HOUSE

I
Cross the threshold
and enter the house
with a throbbing
of light,
this light.
Grieve now for the one holding a long spear
standing at the door of night,
and take him to his loved ones who miss him.

II
Cross the threshold
and enter with steps of happiness.
The promise
has cracked the shell of its parentheses.
Time, that assassin of seasons, bends its frame.
We grew up, then grew old in a glimpse of your
  ankle.

III
Cross the threshold
and say the Lord's name.
At each glimpse of you a flock of doves takes off

whiter than the sleeper's bed,
and each spark of you
guides a lost moon to its orbit.
With your right hand, stamp a palm of henna
 on the arch above the door.
Despite itself, the darkest of dark nights
turns white
when you place a foot on the threshold.

THE SCENT REMINDS

The scent returns to remind,
the same scent
in all that's left behind,
in all that's inhabited
with shadow and aura.

The scent reminds of gifts no one gave,
of beds in rooms drenched in mid-morning light,
of clothes wilting on clothes lines,
of sunrays that break on shoulders,
of the dust of ruins falling on fists,
of breaths trying to find new paths to the highest air,
of the water of bones
spilled on lace,
of loam,
of rams aroused by the scent of urine,
of space explorers taken by the moon's expression,
of the colour of amber,
and lilac
sodden
with rain fallen on mud roofs,
of wheat stored in stables.
The scent reminds of grasses,
of dizziness,
of what's circular and soft,
of the razor sharp,

the scent,
the same scent that ambushes on nights
held by a thread of hallucination.

Let the one watching over the craters
witness the waking of a butterfly.
The scent rises
to nostrils,
a damselfly that
flies among the columns
and falls
on the threshold.
Bring it closer to
the hunter of weakness
among flakes of gold.
Bring it closer
to the fuzz rising from marble skin,
to the stab of myrtle,
to the coronet of a soporific flower,
to whatever returns the mouth to its childhood
and releases the tongue
like a snake.

The scent remains
on the hand
on the nose
on lips
in the folds of breasts

on the curtain
on the emboldened air,
the same scent.

How wonderful when the day's rule retreats,
when obligations fall one after another,
when desires release the tigers at their shoulders
and let them roam the expanses of abandonment.

A ROSE OF BLACK LACE

The pearl in the nose,
the small star of gold
gleams under a straight gaze.
Gloried with freckles,
a nomad of cold climes,
stay away a bit so the air can reach
the mushroom
under the plough.

★

My rains are dry, and your lips are wet.

★

Cold penetrates us from within our own depths.
We tremble because the mist of your freckles
has fallen on our wounds.
My heart trembles from an old chill.

★

Night
is a train pulled by tired bulls,
and the woman spreads her whiteness on the stranger.
White this black-hearted night,
white
treacherous

costly
and tall
wearing a pair of black pumps,
white, and blonde
guarded by sleepless grass,
grass for the tame beast grazing
the plain.
White
gleaming
pulsing
wide-spread,
maker of gasps,
foam white,
and death on a pillow made of tremors.
White
with a birth mark,
with marble,
the white of sapphire,
the white of her turn,
white on the edges of mercury,
of hills without paths to climb them,
a hidden white
wrapped in ribbons
dozing in satin,
white indomitable
white tyrannical
white of sleep and regret
white of clouds raining on beds,

cunning white
that sent us out stripped of our inheritance,
white of lies and obedience
white of supplication and the first showers of rain.
Triumphant white
carrying scents and shivers,
sleeping in his linens,
my little master
who does not rise to the music
of my hand's flutes.
A cone of sugar that melts in saliva,
a lover boy proud of his gold and clothes.
Clean
straight-edged
spread
in the glistening of olive dew,
washed with rains and storm
sending a scent
of grass cut in the morning,
a snake spiralling into the aroma
while the great eye looks on.

★

She lets clothes witness with awe
how an arrow pierces a bird made of sleeves.
She leaves her scent;
she leaves other breaths behind her breathless,
the fingers on the fold of the shirt,

the sweat from hips
erases night's ink
and radiates fever's musk.

★

With a touch
I release the sample out of the mould,
and with the light of gleaming water
I reach for
the origin
of the scream.

★

The rose of black lace

at the nexus of thighs,
the kiss of the happy king
on the thousandth night
when the snake spotted with dew
slid
and began to guard the herb.

★

Silk at the top,
princes jostle under its knots.
Saliva pours.
They reach the jewel

Shepherd of Solitude

prostrate
in supplication,
crawling on their elbows.
I hallucinate my love
and hoard every scrap of air.

★

Show it to me
just aroused from sleep,
bloated with promise,
dew on its crown,
pomegranate seeds
adoring its ears.

★

I want
to see
it
out of its
hiding,
pulling
toward it
all the morning's
dew.

INVOCATION

Your unaware hand on the white knee is white,
the ankle that shines in the night of my eyes is white,
your high shoulders are white
and the broad board of your chest is white,
your wayward doves are white
and the meridian between them is white,
your dome is white, your plain white,
the sleep of narcissus flowers between two oval
  marbles is white,
your thin waist is white
and your bending is white,
your gait is white, its realm white,
your nightgown strewn behind you is white
and your scent in it is white,
your touch is white
and your tiger in bed is white,
your heaving is white
and my white that spills
is white.

THE LOVER'S ASCENT

You were born with this name
so that your memory
is retold by rain showers
that fall
in silence.

With this name
so that travellers will come to you,
lonely
and defeated,
fatigue on their faces from nights spent devoted to
   you.
We return to your hands to drink
from their skill in destruction,
from their defeat of love
whose wound you touch and easily heal.

The wound
of an old
love
stretches
its green
shadows,
wide
as a lover's

regret.

Why don't they stop, these hands pushing us into columns
as we strive to reach the luminous fruit
lit with the incandescence of the deepest depth?

Our eyes are white with happiness
as if we are blind, but we see you through scent
and read your presence with breath.
Our woman,
we failed to learn the way of ether
yet when you raised your hand
we raised ours
though no mirror was to be found.
Your air touched us and wounded us
and we came toward you, all of us, from every direction
and were afraid to be alone.

★

Our table,
our oil,
bread
and salt.

★

You were there

and we did not see you.
We knew you by your scent and the cup you held.
Your servant would refill it later
ignorant of what he touched.
We felt for your traces on the table
and licked your taste on rims
that you left behind.
Virgins came later and enviously
wiped the shadows your fingers left
on the wood.

⁂

Joy to all who see you,
to whoever places his hand on the stone of your knee,
to whoever dips a finger in your navel
and catches the scent of a secret.
Joy to whoever spreads an arm
around your thin waist,
who comes to the stream and drinks his fill.

⁂

Our woman, ours all
gracious at day,
alone in the transparency of night.
You laugh and we fall ill.
You dangle our destinies from eyelashes
and glances fall from you

into fever,
into captivity.

*

We see you on the edge of the bed
wearing your black stockings,
your hair a rainstorm,
your naked back gleaming,
and we fall into a stupor
though we are not
drunk.

Show us your face
so that we look more beautiful in mirrors,
so that we rise above the reed,
so that we trust our limbs
when they are called for work,
so that we are comforted.

*

We possess you, then lose you,
surround you
with branches and spears,
but you trick us,
while your hand softly holds ours.

*

You are our woman,

Shepherd of Solitude

ours all,
born with these eyes to seem other than yourself,
leaning in comfort, surrounded by the sound of
  rustling . . .
You are fruit that strangers split
among themselves. We climb steps
where your air plays with people's heads
and where spears are then broken
on marble.
Proud among our kin
we were duped by a white
magic
gleaming with victory,
by poppy smoke streaming from
your sweet seam.

★

Did we catch the scent of apple
as we ascended?
Did we see Bedouins bearing short swords
cutting a path through the trees?
Did we hear slaves being freed
with the sound of trumpets?
Did we see lovers guiding thieves to a treasure?
Did we win you, deservedly
white
and unharmed,
bearing the joy of those returning

to warm beds in their homes
after a cold, mountainous climb?

*

You,
your name,
the ring of your voice
your kiss
your saliva
your summit and plain
your succulent twigs
your bee and honey
your humility
the she-lion inside you
your mercy
the taste of your salt
your nest
your roc egg
your step
your feet
your toes
your sandals
your precious stone
your marble
the board of your shoulders
your navel
the eye of your navel
your dove

Shepherd of Solitude

your stream
the trickle of your dew
your slumber
the scent of your sleep
your dreams
your brassieres
your trousers
the incense of your limbs
your lightning
your thunder
your prayer for rain
your rain
the scent of the earth after you
your moss
the instinct of flight in the wings of your sparrow hawk
your to and fro
your isthmus
the pain with raised weapons on the fringes of your kingdom
your isthmus
your captives and freed men tossed from your highest tower,
kerchiefs and souvenirs of them –
the night whose dark is beaten by your whiteness
empties his rooms to house guests in its wound –
tattoos from your rituals
the heaven of your heaven

the hell of your hell
that no one tastes
unless longing had planted a palm inside him
and it bore fruit
and he was the first to taste . . .
no one
except for he who brings the gem of confession
from your mouth to his,
except the one who forgets himself
and is remembered by your breath
your cold
your fire
your
salv
a
tion

from *Ascent of Breath*, 1997

Amjad Nasser

FAREWELL TO GRANADA

We will never know how long we dozed there
under the shade of our eyelashes
and how long the earth spun us
in books exchanged among many readers.
But we returned as light as we could be
and we did not find the ones
we had left on the towers
to block the seven winds
as if we had dozed past our age.
Why else would the silhouettes turn dark,
the mountain tops shrivel,
and the letter "aleph" twist
as if the arrow of water lying between two banks
had become the road our allies' ride when they return,
their shoulders sagged with defeat in a border exchange?

★

There is nothing for the date palms to do here
and the songs have nothing to offer the strangers as
   they start their travel.
Our coins are stamped with sleep,
the ringing of our voices stolen by the wind.

★

Here we return to
witness the fate of star and branch
and we see the prince
light
on the earth,
with legs made of cane trying to rouse
the storm.

★

We lifted him a little
heading toward the hill
to incite
a feeling of loss in him
so that he would weep away
houses
and lands
and young sleeping beauties,
virgins lying in the lap of morning light.

Amjad Nasser

SLANT OF DAY

The tall, slender, and envied maiden came walking.
Sister to pure morning
she crossed the meridian of eternity
and turned into an eye for a blind man carving in the air,
a retinue for a prince sleeping under soft linen.
Among her sisters
she was the day's gift to the horizon.
With small feet
she stepped
toward the tolling bells.

In that perfect spring
eulogists and genealogists also came
and players of long flutes
amidst smoke
that screened the stomping of agitated rams.

Not fair-skinned
and without tattoos on her youthful arms,
she had the look of someone
who has promised herself much.
She weighed the air between summit and abyss
and headed with a golden coin between her breasts
toward the one lying awake

guarding his treasure of sleeplessness.

This is her day,
the day her heels strike
the long path of the setting sun.
Ahead of her, bells toll to sanctify
a new hill among towering mountains.
This is the day of sword and laurel crown,
the day pain wraps childhood into memory's folds.
The day a hand reaches for her
and she rises above him,
the one the maidens gaze at
and always see a horse
with an arrow in its chest
and signs of eternity on his brow.
The day when the scent of youth wafts
though it's been stowed like treasure inside
the blades of courtyard grass.
A day of beauty, when the ignorance of those who witness it
is more eloquent than a feast, and closer to their hearts
than their jugular veins.

Slave girls can no longer scheme at night
for she has come, she with the look

that has made dangling fruit drop from branches.
She slept naked on the surface of waking
breathing the air of Seville's orange trees.
Near her lay a snake with a ten-day store of venom.
With her eyes closed
she hoped to receive her share of pain.

★

She, whose name is an invocation,
slowly released her arrow
and struck
the day (in its liver)
playing innocently among the trees.

★

The rustlings
of a delicate prince in frilled capes on the sofa . . .
Those nearest to him
rush to his side with
the same ease
with which they revealed his secrets
in feverish bedchambers,
in the hidden realm
where women rule
with expert cunning.

★

Shepherd of Solitude

Like them, she noted the slant of day
as afternoon light granted the date palm
its fruit clusters from the blood of the two sisters.
With a hand that tames the tiger of breath
she reads the void of the evening through its usual din,
showing the horizon how far the wind must travel
through the trees.

The flood
reached
its peak.
Measures
were even
on the scale.
But she measured
double her worth.

★

The malice
that proffers night
its breast
has fallen apart.

Bones have grown feeble.
Provisions
are all but gone.

★

Entreaty is like rain to him who holds his sword
near the walls,
who stands at the doorstep with key in hand.
He accepts silently what the days bring him
surrounded by the cries of those banished from their
   home.

★

Sunset bears down its weight on the shoulders that
   hold up the day,
the ones leaving the Paradise of the Wise are at the
   mercy of the gales.
And death, in a drowsy mask, is playing in the realm,
throwing his dice, betting on regions in the air.
Among his many voices
he chooses the feeblest.
His groan
beams like a flash
that illuminates
an eagle's sleep
like a fire
on the heights.

A DUSK FORETOLD

The hands that calmed the mountains' surge
are now calming breaths that rise like flames
in houses where baptismal oil is stored.
Grace seeks your pardon.
The holy verses will not sound out again making the
　date palms bow.
The brothers behind the borders are a faraway dream.
The strangers who danced on the shoulders of night
will not raise their voices under the windows of
　Albaicin[4]
The moon is waning to a sliver.
You name is a sign that eyes eschew.
The rhymes that turned drops of dew
into globes in virgin laps
are silent in their books.
Cotton now blossoms out of ears and navels.
The old maids are flitting about groping at the scent
of an old masculinity in priestly robes.
In the dry riverbeds
measles spawns.

You heard endless calls:
the exhales of horses under heavy saddles,

---

[4] A neighbourhood in Granada

the whistling of spurs,
the rumblings of elders,
the wailing of mothers for their eldest sons far away.
The clamour of crowds caught between earth and sky.

For a long time
you heard the creaking of memory
and the hissing of the wind through desire's reeds.

★

Master of this apocalyptic dusk,
I saw in the star that nursed your steps
your silhouette struggling in the wilderness.
You were drying the blood spilled in the hall of the two sisters[5],
cleaning the door handles,
wiping dust off languid panegyrics inscribed on the walls,
sunning the sheets,
drenching the bed of deflowering in incense smoke,
preparing the table,
pacing with feet lost in reverie
on the marble of memory.
There was nothing for you to do

---

5 A hall in the Alhambra Palace in Granada,

but to praise the jutting mountains
fated to surrender their stags.
You've praised the thick air
and exaggerated the height of the trees,
you've praised the melons of your region,
the waters of your springs
that you offered to raucous guests who hoisted
a bloody horizon before your eyes.

The
defeated ones
are set
to leave.
Laughter
in the
balconies
of dusk
rattles the
jaws of
voluptuous
women.

★

You told your vision to no one
where the pirates of sleep came at you one by one
and crowned you king in the affairs of night.
You have roamed cities accompanied

by barbarians and Mudejars[6],
witnessed kingdoms buckling
under the wings of forgetfulness,
princesses shedding their gold
falling from the highest desires.
A call instructed you,
"We exchange days among the living,"
so you gave thanks to mysterious brothers who
filled your cup and overwhelmed you with shifting
   images,
and you gave thanks to guest magicians
trying to subdue insomnia
sealing the cracks in the night
with the wax of wakefulness.

With huge hands they guarded your last sigh
and with leopard-like shapes they awaited the
   refugees.
The sign
of the past
belongs
to the
ferocity

---

[6] Mudejar refers to non-Arab Muslim converts of Andalusia who lived under Christian rule before and during the Christian reconquest of Spain. The Arabic origin of the word "Mudajar" is *mudajan*, which means "domesticated".

of dusk.
You heard silhouettes narrate the lives of the ancestors
to immigrants who chronicle the habits of anxiety
and who write the book
of forces that will never reconcile

With the same hands that surrendered sword and key
you held a flute and began to slash the ghosts
that multiply in sleep.
They are your lowly cousins
who have settled with women who sway
between hovels and cages in the dregs of night.
They settled among conquerors who silenced the tribes,
gave them a lineage in the hinterlands,
and forced them to change their names.

ASCENT OF BREATH

I

Neither the spears of the mighty, nor the knives of dwarves
but
your hand,
rather
the fingers of your hand;
no,
your breath
tearing furrows through eternal air,
leaving them to be seeded with pain carried from tooth to tongue.
I hear them beyond the incense
of poppy, luring the idols of my life,
spreading their palms at the doorstep.
I climb their path, hoisting my confusion as a flag
of surrender to the gales.

II

Not with sword
or diamonds,
but with breath,

he or she
tempted me
away from the summit of my alertness,
tempted me,
I, whose back was
supported by the hardiness of my lineage and my invocations.

>All of night was left to me . . .
>insomnia followed by air
>stabbed with moaning.

I fell the way a clown falls, happy in his nimbleness.
My lineage will not return me to my status among the tribes
and my eyes could not waver from the abyss
that lured me with its bells.
Breaths
slid off
their veils,
the hard
air
pulled me toward it,
my right to rule the realms
waved
its alarm.

III

Like a captive jolted awake
by the turmoil of a startled night
I heard the sound of steps
repeating the small breaths
of rustling fabric.
A silhouette of plumes touched me and I saw your apparition
pouring light on the dark side,
and promising a endless night,
sprinkling its signs
on whomever catastrophe chooses among the duped.
I took off all my earthly implements and said, "I am now light."
Through the boughs I detected traces of your bare feet passing
on the grass, not with my eyes but with my heart's tremors.
I marched on into the land seeking you. I refused
the trackers' wisdom and sought your presence.

IV

On the hill of regret
I denied my birth star
and shed the skill that distinguished me from my peers.

Among the wide shoulders going past
I was the figure bent beneath lightning.
I turned to slopes that silently received the summits' sermons.
Then below a deaf sky I heard the elements splitting apart
at the height of their abandonment.
I came upon hills being born of the mountains' amnesia
and spirits floating tattooed by the horseshoe of midday heat.
I passed boxthorn spreading aimlessly along the paths
and I turned to my brother,
and with what strength I mustered I grabbed a fistful from the soil
that harboured seeds of poison and elixir.
Crowds gathered and the dust raised a veil between us.
They returned with spoils of nothingness.
I resorted to a mountain hoping to snatch
a share of what could be seen.

V

Did I see, or was it what fever projected?
Longings waved their lanterns
at people crossing the dark nights of their souls
and who would never reach their beds.

I saw forgiveness hosting brigands who fled the
   remains of their names.
I saw brotherhood spread between two giants who
   horrified the realms,
clouds shade an orphan abandoned by his kin,
and the treasure guarded by seven ghosts reveal itself.

On that loose evening,
a dying hope held by your captive
retrieved its vigour
when your hand
ascended
and touched
my hand,
and I began to see.

VI

"The heart cannot belie what it sees,"

nor the eye that I graced with forgiveness
and let guard the shadows of those who passed,
nor the hand that brought me news of my lower limbs;
or the smell of cardamom that accompanied me
       (wherever I went I gave away a secret
       that
       I knew

    less than anyone),
nor my breath that gave you your body
and that climbed slowly from my soles to my scalp
and almost abandoned me when your heaven began
  to loom.

Not a single drop of a daisy's blood has ever lied.
  It fell
  and conjured
  a dusk
  that will never
  heal.

VII

. . . But
why won't this glass
and that smoke
not release me from the grip of insomnia?
Why do I
not drift away
or waken
as though I had not seen
or heard
or touched
or inhaled your breath
upon my hands?

VIII

It's not the magi's star
or fire lit by my kin tonight
that burns
and captures,
but
your silhouette
passing
between two summits,
or perhaps your breaths
luring promises that do not live or die,
or perhaps my regret
tossing balls of flame
from the vastness of the night
to measure the depth
of the abyss.

IX

Lighter than a hope on a mountain of despair,
like a feather that flees the quagmire of a wing,
and heavier than me in the palm of the wind –
my soul
is inclined to suffer,
like my thirsty lips at the edge of the stream,

my hands
set their traps
and return empty.

X

I am crowned with lightness.
My throne is in the air
held by tormented breath.
My lightness left no trace of me on the ground,
but it did not lift me to you.
O my lightness,
raise me
or drop me with a bent shoulder
to repel the dust erasing the traces of
 my childhood among the pomegranate trees.

O my lightness,
the stranger arrived
with a yesterday or a tomorrow,
the stranger
has arrived
on his
last
breath.

from *Life Like A Broken Narrative*, 2004

THE HOUSE AFTER HER DEATH

Nothing has changed after my mother's death.
Her portraits are still youthful. My four sisters are
    still intent on keeping the day tied to
its three stalwart rituals: coffee in the mornings,
    ginger at midday, mint in the evenings.
At my family's home you do not need a watch.
The scent will tell you the sun's place in the sky.

Nothing has changed in that house since my
    mother's death.
My sisters' hands keep busy tidying up the rooms
    their five brothers have left for other rooms
in which their souls will never rest.
They no longer sleep on mattresses spread on the
    floor,
no longer shiver like addicts while they wait for
    their morning tea and bread.

After my mother's death, nothing has changed in
    the house.
When we look at Kawthar, our oldest sister, intent
    on keeping even small things whole,
we begin to think that our mother hasn't left the
    house she built, sigh by sigh,
in a white coffin and a body eaten bit by bit

by cancer, for a graveyard to hold the first of the
   family dead.

Nothing has changed after my mother's death:
the day with its three degrees of latitude,
the tidy rooms awaiting absent sons,
my father's endless marathon racing between
   ablutions and the mosque,
the everlasting nostalgia for the happy days of our
   poverty.

Everything is still the same
except for that hand which turns the dust green.

OLD RADIO

To see just what had enthralled me then, I looked through the storage room (home of things that neither die nor live) for the books that led me to flee the country. That's where I found it: the old radio, a Phillips, with the green eye that shone through my father's sleepless nights.

It stood silent, tattered, stripped of its rank as the most important member of the household.

The fine mesh that had poured out emotions, intrigues, and lies is broken. The thick black leather is cracked. The old stations (London, Washington, Berlin, Moscow, Tirana) that stirred peoples and trouble in the East with long harangues, are quiet as gravestones covered in dust.

My father, a tank corps officer, warned me never to move the needle too fast, fearing I'd set it loose from its fixed orbit in the universe. It stood frozen at Radio Damascus, which the family only tuned to during Ramadan to hear the child-voice of Sheikh Tawfiq al-Munjid.

. . . .

I did not find my secret books. My family probably got rid of them soon after I left. And they were right, for who in Mafraq had any need for *The German Ideology* or *What is To Be Done?*? I found my stifled adolescence there when I was stuck and barely living on rapacious daydreams. The Babylonian sounds that rose and spread reclaimed a life lived only in songs.

A YOUNG WOMAN IN COSTA CAFÉ

Morning light, at Costa Café in Hammersmith,
burns vainly, hoping to catch some more from
London's effaced sky.

She comes in, sits at the table opposite me, though
the café is empty. I am there thinking about a
poem in which a young woman steps into a café
and sits opposite a poet trying to write a poem
about a young woman who enters an empty café
and sits opposite him.

She puts her books on the table, her bag on the
floor. Raindrops fall as she removes her red leather
coat. Looking in my direction, she thrusts her firm
breasts outward, and they sway inside her blouse.

When she leans over her bag, her hair hangs loose,
and with a hasty motion she pushes it back. She
lights a cigarette, begins sipping her coffee and
looks at me from the corner of her eye. She moves
her head as if about to say something, but does
not. More than once I want to say something too,
but hold back.

She looks like the young woman in that poem: her

blue short-sleeved blouse revealing shapely
forearms, shoulders from which a little leopard
leapt, her legs moving under the table like a pair of
fans.

All signs lead to her.

The weight and movement of the air begin to
change under the table. As if by accident, I drop
my pen to the ground to see what might be going
on under hers. By the time I retrieve the pen and
raise my head she is gone.
There, on the wall in front of me, hangs a huge
poster of a young woman sitting alone, smoking
and sipping her coffee, gazing out of the corner of
her eye in a café just like this one.

. . . .
. . . .

The disturbed air is still blowing under the table.
The hot cup of coffee.
The burned-out cigarette on the edge of the
ashtray.
The lipstick-smeared tissue.
My heart, its beating audible from afar.
The poem I thought of, but that someone else
wrote.

SEVEN BRIDGES

To my brother Ahmad

When we used to stop at Seven Bridges and look
at the gravel-covered valley that has no name
(where there is no water, there is no name), we
did not know that one day I would find my way
to London Bridge and you to Brooklyn Bridge.

No one who knew Seven Bridges (the miracle of
Zarqa suspended in ellipses of dust) had ever heard
of those two bridges or thought there were
bridges more awesome than this one with its
seven arches that the Ottomans built to lay the
Hijaz railroad in the last gasp of their janissary
reign.

Gusts of wind pumped under it.
Birds of prey made their nests
      in its crevices.
Women placed charms for their husbands
      between its stones.
Night had assigned it
      to be the keeper of its darkness.

Remember how we used to throw coins
and they rusted

before hitting the ground,
how we threw a shirt the wind tore in two,
a green branch that instantly turned into charcoal.

But faraway in the cold country of England that
now implores the rain god to raise his palms a
little, there was a bridge (immortalised by an
American-born English poet named Eliot) that
joined London's two muddy riverbanks.
Sleepwalkers crossed it to castles of money, and
many suicides bowed their heads from it and
threw themselves away. On the other shore of the
Atlantic (where Bedouin intuition is useless) was a
more impressive bridge called the Brooklyn. All
the tribes of Jordan can cross that bridge without
a single screw coming loose.

Seven Bridges. My father threatened (in your
presence, perhaps) to throw me off of it if I did
not stop smoking, and stealing from neighbouring
gardens, or chasing girls and entering our house
by climbing over the stone fence and not through
the front door. My heart was falling and not
reaching bottom as he put his big hand over the
nape of my neck showing me how far down the
ground was. All the bridges I have seen since have
not shaken it from my memory.

Shepherd of Solitude

It was not the height,
or the gravel floor,
or the grave of Um Youssef Saleem,
the first of our dead on the other hill,
but the three Ottoman shell cases
I found with the Jinaah street gang,
filled with gold Majeedi coins (according to me)
and filled with spoilt gunpowder (according to
the police) . . .

Twenty years after a mythical flight, while eyes
trapping blue flies watched,
I sat on the edge of Seven Bridges and was afraid
to dangle my feet and reveal the distance
between my memory and the ground below.

SOUVENIR

The bullet he shot out of his father's (paratrooper) pistol, while playing under an arc of heat and boredom, and that almost killed his younger brother, lodging itself in the middle drawer of the family's first wardrobe, that same bullet was left there (probably deliberately) as a souvenir of the family's eldest who left vowing to never return.

THE RING FROM KAIROUAN

I

Ever since I saw this ring in the hand of the poet Saadi Youssef, I was captivated by it.

On that night in the Salutation pub I tried to avoid looking at it, but could not. Saadi must have noticed my fidgeting and that my torso was leaning forward toward his right hand, where the ring was perhaps spewing its fumes through the crack in its crown. I told Saadi that I admired his ring and he took it off and gave it to me, mumbling something like "what the old pass on to the young". It is difficult sometimes to ascertain exactly what Saadi says, especially when he, for some reason, begins to take the shape of the porcupine of his famous poem.

But this is not the beginning nor the end of this ring's story. It had belonged to a Sufi from Kairouan who had nothing else of value when he died. Perhaps it is the ring of sainthood. The Sufi passed it on to his son who followed in his father's footsteps until he heard Saadi recite his poetry one night in Kairouan. He especially loved a poem titled "The Ancestors" and to express his admiration to the poet he offered his only valuable possession to Saadi. The poet, famous for his seven stutters, stood confused, unsure of what to do with a snub-nosed silver ring that had a crack on its crown.

II

A year after acquiring the ring I found myself in Southall, the west London fortress of South Asians in England, exposing my senses to the aromas of the East so that they remain alert, and so that I do not end up buried by mistake in Greenford Cemetery, for example. That's when I went into a jeweller's and asked for the ring to be repaired.

The Indian jeweller asked me if I was sure that I wanted to weld the crack on the ring and I answered affirmatively.

He welded it as much as he could.

Soon the ring became too tight for my right ring finger, so I switched it to my left where it was too wide and kept slipping off. The shape of the ring changed; it was no longer snub-nosed. The

etchings that I thought were calligraphy
disappeared. I would give up all of my poetry to
know what those etchings said. Were they a
riddle that I had to answer and failed to? Or a
message that I never bothered to read?

I began to wake up in the morning without the
normal urges that pricked me like lightning,
those expectations and hummings, those foolish
promises I made to myself. My hair began to go
grey all of a sudden and I had no signs of wisdom
to show for it, none of that impressive silence, or
the renouncement of the rat race for status and
fame.

I realised too late
that I had committed a grave violation.
Alas, if only I could know what it was!

DOG'S TAIL

My mother died in 2000 after she learned that all the clocks and calendars had changed, and possibly after she heard about something called "the millennium". But she, who was illiterate and who did not need to handle complex numbers, knew, perhaps because she was preparing to depart, that the world she left behind would not be any different with a change of clocks and calendars. Her guide in this regard was her favourite Bedouin proverb. In this story, a dog's tail is placed in a mould to straighten it and it emerges as crooked as it had ever been when it is pulled out forty years later – a parable, which it so happens, perfectly encapsulated my mother's opinion of me.

SOMETHING LIKE ANGER, LIKE BETRAYAL

Even after all these years an anger that resembles betrayal fills him when he remembers her. The emotions that blazed then extinguished, and the expectations that were fulfilled then floundered, would not shake that cursed feeling from him.

What would have happened if he hadn't told her that he could not continue their relationship because he could not look, without averting his eyes, at his child's silent and persistent stares? The boy was trying to discern his father's plans, after frequent absences from home, and now that the parents slept in separate rooms. He wanted to know why he was now going to school with his father or mother, and not with the two of them holding him, each by a hand, and swinging him the whole way through grade school with the strength of the enzymes of their familial bliss.

Seriously, he thought, what would have happened had he not told her about all this?

Would she have moved after her impending divorce, as they'd planned in exact details, from

her city "N" to his city "L," to be with him
twenty-four hours a day, no space or time
separating them, to gulp without ever being sated
by the springs of their love that burst out of each
exchanged look, touch, or embrace – their love,
which no poetry had yet written of, and whose
lightness no song had yet hummed?

Nothing has remained of that love. Sometimes he
failed even to remember her face.

But his faltering memory (of this!) still easily
entraps him with the smell of her perfumes, the
colour of her underwear, the shapes of her shoes,
the inventive positions she took when they made
love.

The anger, or to be precise, let's say the sense of
betrayal, that accompanies him now is not because
the springs of their love had dried up too quickly,
but because she accepted the news of their
separation without shock, as if he had not flung a
bomb at her feet that was to shake the world and
all that inhabited it.

After a short while, a month or less than a month,
scenes of their lovemaking, which he had not
experienced with any other woman, began to

shake off their brief hibernation. And he asked a mutual friend about her.

She told him that his beloved was having a blazing love affair with some man.
"Another man?"
"Yes!"
"Do I know him?"
"Perhaps?"
"Is it A?"

She looked at him with laughing, mischievous eyes, and did not answer.
He didn't ask how it happened.
He only needed to remember that he was the one who gave her, when love had anesthetised the wolf within him, A's phone number in case she needed anything in her city of "N."

But when?
When?
This is the question!

PREPARING FOR FLIGHT

It was not old age, not even forgetfulness, but a desire to unburden herself from the faces, the voices, the details (for they are the source of the earth's gravity) that led her to prepare for flight.

Was that not the reason she let threads slip from her hands and hang there dangling? Yes, she was saving her energy for the last leap that would untie all the knots that linked her to the faces, voices, and tiresome details.

I could not find another explanation for my grandmother's refusal to remember me when I sat beside her in a dusk that crawled like forgetfulness on the verandah of our house in Mafraq.

Time, that slow poison, which had increased its doses to her loved ones, had promised her very little. Still, she continued to wrestle with an existence she would otherwise be the first to forego.

Because I crouched on the ground close to her so that she could not avoid me, she asked who I was.

"I am Yahya."
"But Yahya is in America."
"That's Ahmad, my brother. I am Yahya and I live in Britain."
"God destroy them both! Lands of filth!"

With her head pointed to the stars, which she forbade us from counting so that warts would not grow on our hands, she seemed to remember me and at last said, "So, you have come."

I told her that I came every year, but without my children this time.

"But you have no children."
"That's Ahmad. I am Yahya and I am married to Hind the Lebanese. You know her. I have a daughter and a son."

She struck her head lightly, apologising for the mix-up, laughing for the first time from behind her thick glasses that looked like ancient telescopes, especially when she raised her head to the sky (which she did often).

"Right, right, I have grown forgetful, my grandchild."

She told the story of how I had feigned illness
one hot day and made her carry me on her back
from the Zarqa reservoir to our house in the army
campground. And when we arrived I began to
jump like a chimpanzee with my friends.

"I must have got better," I said, feeling happy that
she had finally caught the thread that belongs to
me from among the jumbled weave of her ninety
years.

My father entered the room holding the cordless
phone and told me my brother was on the line.
After I finished the call, she asked me who I was
talking to.

"Ahmad."

And as if I was playing a silly game that had lasted
longer than it should, she looked indignantly at
me and said,

"Then who are you?"

A RESEMBLANCE

I was slurping a mug of cold beer on a hot summer day when I kept hearing someone loudly huffing at his cigarette and striking his hand on the table. He was telling his friend that the women he had stuck with over the years, in his indefatigable search for love, were the ones who refused him or let him go.

The first was the neighbours' girl who rejected him despite his willingness to slit his arteries for her. Though she opted for a young, muscle-bound baker who had a fierce-looking mane, he never forgot her. He saw her several times, walking with slumped shoulders, leading a platoon of children who hopped around her like ducklings. (They must be the progeny of that cursed baker).

As for the second one, she left a bitter taste in him (a taste that was never shaken from his throat), after such sweet kisses that he now suspects could never have happened. How could she have refused him before cockcrow while saliva from her desired mouth still wetted his lips?

The tone of his last words struck a bell within my depths. My ears turned and widened like radar dishes.

She was a flight attendant working for a foreign airline.
He met her in this very bar. He had a friend with him, a player, who proved much more wily than he. He wished he had never introduced him to her and that he was not with him on the day that's now engraved on the slates of eternity.

I stopped caring for the story when I predicted its end.

But the voice is what sculpted me like a two-headed statue into my seat.
It was the same voice,
the same timbre dripping with sorrow,
the same fist that banged fiercely on the table,
the same story that leaves a bitter taste in the throat.

I feared to turn around and see myself.

PUPPY DOG

Here you are seated in front of her carelessly,
crooking your tail this way, sprawling your long
legs that way.

Everything is normal, the young face pulled
tight on rare marble is no surprise, the hands
that call out with ten violins are a cause for
boredom and nothing else. The taut stomach
that stares at eternity with the mystery of its
navel . . .

I am in the chair behind you.
I see you with your own eyes twenty years later.
Your hands render her pleading hands worthless
on the table
and dangle and loll here and there.
Your empty eyes graze all the surrounding faces
in this droning bar, avoiding hers. When they
fail to snare any sign from any direction you sink
deeper into your seat as she tries with all her
gifts to shake a response out of you, to no avail.

Now
in your age
and with your face insolent

before all the miracles that display their truths
before you,
you, you puppy dog, will not know what you
have lost except by sitting in the chair just behind
yours.

THE PHASES OF THE MOON IN LONDON

She and I were talking about the weather, the rusty key that opens conversations here in London. Mrs. Morrison, our old neighbour, is the last English woman on our street, where the English have dropped off one by one since the population balance tipped toward the Asian immigrants. She said, "the London sky was not like this in the past, but must have resembled your sky in India."

I said, "I am from Jordan," but she did not stop at my correction, which she may not have seen as a correction in the first place. In that English manner whose emotional resonances are hard to read, she continued that they too used to see the stars and detect the phases of the moon.

I was not convinced, but I played on in this game of English politeness. I said, "What caused the stars and moon to disappear and the sky to turn into a blotted sheet even on these nights clear as a rooster's eye?"

"I don't know," she said. "Maybe the change in

the weather, or our insatiable consumption of electricity, this excessive urbanization. We light the earth and the sky disappears. You're probably better off in India."

"In Jordan," I said.

Again, she did not pause at my correction. She smiled and directed her small shopping trolley toward her house, announcing the end of a conversation that politeness had imposed on two neighbours who otherwise try all they can to avoid each other when they meet at the door.

I wanted to tell her that the skies of eastern cities, bent under military rule and corruption, are also blotted out, and that the stars that freckled our childhood with comets have also disappeared, but I feared to lose the only gift for which she envied me.

AN ORDINARY CONVERSATION ABOUT CANCER

(For Salih al-Azzaz)

Whenever we remembered a departed friend we also remembered it was cancer that took him.

"Does anyone these days die of anything except cancer, that cursed hunter of reveries?"

I said this to a friend who had told me about another friend upon whom cancer had crept as he was contemplating a theory of desert life. Our friend suddenly felt an unusual headache and was taken to hospital, where they found a tumor in full command of his brain. After it was removed, he was subjected to chemotherapy, which sheared his scalp, eyebrows and eyelashes and left him looking like an ill infant. Staring at those around him, he died silently, still not believing this whole affair, that started with "a slightly excessive" headache. It pulled him into himself, while outwardly he was fit and full-limbed.

My friend fell silent, then said, "Did you know that my older brother died of cancer at forty?"

I told him about my mother, and how cancer had ambushed her twice: once at fifty, but it withdrew allowing her ten more years. She then wrestled with it for seven months without any detectable hope. "The problem – I don't remember where I read about it – is that a person dies the way his close relatives die," I added.

I thought I saw him touch his head and assured him that since he'd passed forty this rule probably no longer applied to him. As for me, the possibility is still tuning its strings before me.

He asked me how I'd like to die.

From a heart attack, I said, asleep on my bed, and in the morning they find me dead.

He agreed, saying that a heart attack was the quickest and least humiliating way of dying. He didn't have the courage of his brother, who had refused chemotherapy, kept his full head of hair and smoked and drank until his last gasp.

My friend fell silent again, slightly longer this time. "Are you sure people die the way their close relative die?"

"I am not sure," I answered.

★

I am also not sure that poets can prophecy their death, even though Cesar Vallejo died in Paris on a rainy day, exactly as he predicted in his poem "White Stone, Black Stone". I predict in this poem that I will die in London on a rainy day (what a far-fetched prophecy!). And I decree that I be buried in Mafraq next to my mother, who was convinced that no space would ever contain us both. Of course, she may be right, since as everyone knows, she is going to heaven.

NEIGHBOURS

1

The people of Spring Grove Crescent did not need to see the sign in italicised red letters saying "SOLD" to realise that Mrs Morrison, the only Englishwoman in our neighbourhood, had just moved. It was enough to see her windows without their white curtains, which in the past, opening slightly every now and then, would let you know that the old woman persisted at her daily work of keeping a wary eye for those who roamed the streets without any purpose, or those who would obliviously park in front of her doorway in the spot reserved for her only daughter – a daughter who would come only on Saturdays, accompanied by a fat husband carrying a case of beer.

Those of us whose houses ringed the cul-de-sac became certain of her departure by peeking at her garden, which used to be trimmed like the moustache of her late husband who had died of cancer two years before (his moustache went back to the last days of the British Empire). Soon after she left, the lush plants in her garden began to disappear one after the other, like the English from west London.

2

The only problem Mrs Morrison and I had – not
to mention that I used to unintentionally lean too
hard on her wooden fence, and that the smell of
barbeque on rare summer days used to waft from
my garden to hers – the only problem was that I
could never convince her I was not from India
but from a place that never offers any good news
about the shape of the world. After that day,
September 11th, I was thankful for my failure in
this regard. It shielded me from her alert but
invisible eyes behind the white curtains.

3

Mrs Morrison was not her name. I called her that
so that I'd have a name for the side of the bed I
slept on, between her and Mrs Sharma on that
cul-de-sac, barren of stars. I never knew her
name, despite our regular exchanges of
pleasantries from our respective doorways. We
always envied her garden, which stood between
us, we who only thought of cattle and sheep
whenever we saw a patch of green.

The few Christmas cards we exchanged were
addressed "To Next Door Neighbour".

Amjad Nasser

THE STARS OF LONDON

One breath after another, the days shove me forward. Lagging behind, my eyes still hunt for the sign that appeared to me as I lay on the rooftop of our house one night in Mafraq. I was counting the stars when the sign appeared to me, careless that warts would burst through my hands for measuring the sky's bounty.

My eyes have trailed that sign ever since. It is said to point to a spring that leads to a slope where there is a bough and a snake. Under the bough there's a key. The key is for a dark room never to be opened. In it there is a box with a shell inside. In the shell there is a piece of paper saying, "Do not look for me in what looks like me, in shape or surface, for all that is shaped like me is not me, and what looks like me is not myself. I am not close or distant. My sign is nearer to you than your own jugular vein."

One day I saw this vision and forgot the sign. Or was this told to me by a passer-by inserting a needle in another needle's eye? Was he the one who spent a night in my family home and left, never to be seen again?

Shepherd of Solitude

Every night I rest my head on the pillow in vain. I empty my eyes from the spoils of the day, and I cleanse my heart from the moss of a false pulse, all in hope of luring that intractable sign.

In a popular café in Old Fez, in another time or in another life, I may have heard a Moroccan saying to his agitated friend:
Don't look for the sign.
Don't stand in its way.
Don't go rummaging for it in ruins and craters.
Don't chase after stars that have misguided lovers and
 shepherds before you.
The sign does not come to you from where you
 expect,
and not in any way that you can imagine.

In London I live wearing the face of an imaginary person, fleeing my mother's prophecy in which my given name rings like a disturbing memory. "Yahya," she said, "your soul will never reach comfort." And of course, she was right. Here it is nearly impossible to lie on the slanted roof of your house, trying to count the stars that have deserted their posts.